PREFACE

1. Scope

This publication provides joint doctrine for the planning, execution, and assessment of joint operations in an urban environment.

2. Purpose

This publication has been prepared under the direction of the Chairman of the Joint Chiefs of Staff (CJCS). It sets forth joint doctrine to govern the activities and performance of the Armed Forces of the United States in joint operations and provides the doctrinal basis for interagency coordination and for US military involvement in multinational operations. It provides military guidance for the exercise of authority by combatant commanders and other joint force commanders (JFCs) and prescribes joint doctrine for operations, education, and training. It provides military guidance for use by the Armed Forces in preparing their appropriate plans. It is not the intent of this publication to restrict the authority of the JFC from organizing the force and executing the mission in a manner the JFC deems most appropriate to ensure unity of effort in the accomplishment of the overall objective.

3. Application

a. Joint doctrine established in this publication applies to the Joint Staff, commanders of combatant commands, subunified commands, joint task forces, subordinate components of these commands, and the Services.

b. The guidance in this publication is authoritative; as such, this doctrine will be followed except when, in the judgment of the commander, exceptional circumstances dictate otherwise. If conflicts arise between the contents of this publication and the contents of Service publications, this publication will take precedence unless the CJCS, normally in coordination with the other members of the Joint Chiefs of Staff, has provided more current and specific guidance. Commanders of forces operating as part of a multinational (alliance or coalition) military command should follow multinational doctrine and procedures ratified by the United States. For doctrine and procedures not ratified by the United States, commanders should evaluate and follow the multinational command's doctrine and procedures, where applicable and consistent with US law, regulations, and doctrine.

For the Chairman of the Joint Chiefs of Staff:

DAVID L. GOLDFEIN, Lt Gen, USAF
Director, Joint Staff

Intentionally Blank

SUMMARY OF CHANGES
REVISION OF JOINT PUBLICATION 3-06
DATED 08 NOVEMBER 2009

- Expands the discussion on considerations for air operations in urban areas.

- Updates the chapter on understanding the urban operational environment.

- Revises the considerations of physical factors for urban operational areas.

- Realigns operational planning considerations in urban areas.

- Clarifies the joint intelligence preparation of the operational environment process.

- Expands the discussion related to lines of effort considerations in urban areas.

- Revises and updates discussions on special operations capabilities in accordance with existing joint doctrine publications.

- Updates the discussion related to military information support operations.

- Consolidates and updates the section outlining joint fire support.

- Expands the discussion of legal considerations in urban areas.

- Expands the appendix on maritime considerations in support of urban operations.

Intentionally Blank

TABLE OF CONTENTS

APPENDIX

GLOSSARY

FIGURE

EXECUTIVE SUMMARY
COMMANDER'S OVERVIEW

- **Introduces Unique Challenges of Planning and Execution of Joint Urban Operations**

- **Discusses Understanding the Urban Operational Environment**

- **Addresses Planning for Joint Urban Operations**

- **Explains Joint Urban Operations in the Context of Joint Function**

Introduction

This joint publication focuses on capabilities and tasks that are unique to, or significantly challenged by, urban environments at the operational level.

Joint urban operations (JUOs) are joint operations planned and conducted on, or against objectives within, a topographical complex and its adjacent natural terrain, where man-made construction or the density of population are the dominant features. Commanders and their staffs should consider the complex and dynamic interactions and relationships of the population with the physical terrain and infrastructure.

Urban Environment

Urban areas present a complex environment for military operations. This complexity is derived from numerous factors such as location, history, economic development, climate, available building materials, the natural terrain on which they are built, the cultures of their inhabitants, and many other factors. There are many ways to frame an understanding of the factors influencing the urban environment, one of which is to view the urban environment as an urban triad consisting of complex man-made physical terrain, a population of significant size and density and varying sociocultural groupings, and an infrastructure.

Characteristics of Joint Operations in Urban Environments

A few characteristics of joint operations in urban environments are:

- Cities may reduce the advantages of the technologically superior force;
- Ground operations can become manpower-intensive;
- Operations are time-consuming;
- Combat operations in urban areas may result in large ratios of civilian to military casualties; and

	• Operations conducted in urban areas may have more restrictive operational limitations than operations elsewhere.
Air Operations Considerations	Air operations must adapt to the unique urban environment. The urban environment includes challenges such as combat identification, propensity for collateral damage, preservation of infrastructure, restrictive rules of engagement, line of sight obstructions (to include targeting and communications), and freedom of maneuver.
Conditions for Urban Engagement	Operations in urban areas may occur within the context of a campaign or major operation. The joint force commander (JFC) will determine whether or not operating in an urban environment is essential for the conduct of the campaign or major operation and, if so, where and when to conduct JUOs.
Fundamentals of Operations in Urban Environments	The entire urban environment must be addressed simultaneously and systematically by applying power to disable hostile elements and enable those environmental elements that are essential to the city's functioning. A comprehensive and systematic approach requires a combination of isolating, protective, improving, sustaining, persuasive, destructive, and disruptive actions or capabilities.

Understanding the Urban Operational Environment

General	By understanding key aspects of the operational environment through a systems perspective, the JFC and joint planners can then choose dynamic ways to achieve operational objectives. It is important to note, the complexity of the urban environment increases the possibility and incidence of undesired effects or unforeseen consequences from any military operation.
Political	Unique to JUOs is the requirement to influence political/civil institutions in order to shape outcomes to meet the United States Government's (USG's) desired end state. In conjunction with other USG entities, the JFC needs to plan for what elements, to what degree, and to what standards, the JFC will shape the political landscape in accordance with achieving US goals.
Economic	Providing economic assistance in a JUO is a difficult and complicated task that requires coordination and

synchronization throughout the economic area of influence. It is not the job of the military to restore public services or incomes to prewar or other desired levels; that is the job of the citizens of the host nation themselves. It is, however, part of the mission of personnel engaged in joint operations to help create the security conditions that can make growth and development possible.

Special Social and Cultural Considerations for Urban Areas

Understanding local cultural, political, social, economic, and religious factors is crucial to successful JUOs and becomes central to mission success. Relationships between groups might be congenial, hostile, or dependent. Understanding this diversity and complexity requires a significant amount of mental effort and flexibility.

Information Considerations for Urban Areas

Information is the pervasive backdrop of the urban environment. It is continuously changing and requires that plans and operational decisions be based on this knowledge and on the results of constant monitoring, assessment, and analysis.

Infrastructure Considerations for Urban Areas

The total functioning of an urban area is supported by infrastructure which is itself composed of systems. Each component of infrastructure affects the population, the normal operation of the city, and the nature and long-term success of JUOs. Commanders and their staffs should understand the functions and interrelationships of these systems in order to achieve success.

Planning

Planning for operations that will be conducted in urban environments generally follows the same basic process as planning for operations in other environments.

The challenges inherent in operating in an urban area are sufficiently different and complex, requiring commanders and their staffs to give due consideration to the unique requirements of the urban environment. If a major JUO is undertaken as part of a larger campaign, then plans should address the difficult balance, synchronization, and integration between the JUO and the rest of the campaign—including differences in force requirements, tempo of operations, types and quantity of fires and munitions, types and amounts of logistic support, civil-military operations requirements, incident response, and many other areas.

The Strategic and Operational Context

The strategic and operational context of operations conducted in urban environments is multifaceted to include the integration of government policies as well as the execution of tactical-level tasks. The decision to conduct a combat operation within an urban area must have a specific tie to the overall end state.

Operational Art and Operational Design

When planning an operation or campaign to deal with adversaries within urban environments, the JFC must go beyond the idea of attacking the embedded adversary. The entire urban environment must be treated comprehensively, applying power to disable hostile elements and enabling those elements that are essential to the city's functioning. The reality of the urban environment presents a unique set of circumstances and parameters, which will significantly influence the approach to operational art. Commanders at all levels must fit the execution of short-term operations into a larger operational design, and this design must link their near-term actions to the end state.

Phasing

JUOs can normally be divided into phases to logically organize a campaign's or operation's diverse, extended, and dispersed activities. Considerations for shaping, deterrence, and seizing the initiative in urban areas will only differ slightly from those of military operations conducted in other environments.

Other Operation Considerations for Urban Areas

Other operational considerations for JUO include special operations, foreign consequence management; and foreign humanitarian assistance.

Joint Functions

Command and Control

The ability of the JFC to influence the outcome of operations conducted in urban areas is the result of leadership and the ability to control forces and functions in order to execute the intent. The nature of the urban environment accentuates the challenges to the JFC, and offers significant hindrances to effective command and control.

Intelligence

Numerous factors make joint intelligence preparation of the operational environment (JIPOE) for urban areas a complex and detailed undertaking, including the nature of the urban environment. Attaining situational awareness, visualizing operations, and providing timely intelligence and information to support decision making are critical JIPOE functions in an urban environment.

Fires

Fires play a key role in JUOs. In the case of operations involving combat, the JFC can use fires to shape the operational environment and to engage the adversary, but perhaps the most important use of fires is in the isolation of the urban area or points within the urban area. Precision munitions make attacks on specific urban targets much more feasible and effective, although their precision does not reduce or mitigate all risk.

Movement and Maneuver

The physical terrain of most urban areas makes the movement of large forces difficult, even in times of peace and stability. The urban environment significantly affects the ability of the joint force to maneuver by canalizing, increasing vulnerability, reducing options, and slowing movement. Coordinated and integrated horizontal and vertical maneuver in the urban area can slow the defender's ability to react and use interior lines.

Protection

Although protection will not ensure the success of operations in urban areas, failure to take adequate protection measures can cause an operation to fail. The protection function focuses on conserving the joint force's fighting potential.

Sustainment

Operations in urban areas normally will require more of many types of resources (e.g., personnel, munitions, subsistence, medical support) than other operations. Commanders must make every effort to anticipate and specifically plan for these resources. It is important for the JFC to clearly specify appropriate supporting and supported relationships to ensure that subordinate commanders conducting JUOs will have sufficient forces and means.

CONCLUSION

This publication provides joint doctrine for the planning, execution, and assessment of joint operations in an urban environment.

Intentionally Blank

CHAPTER I
INTRODUCTION

"Urban warfare, fighting in cities, war in 'complex terrain.' To the casual observer, the words seem detached, almost pristine. However, the words are strikingly real to military professionals who have seen the images of great destruction and excessive casualties in cities such as Berlin, Stalingrad, Hue, and Beirut. Urban warfare, a subject that many military professionals would prefer to avoid, is still with us. Moreover, it may be the preferred approach of future opponents."

**Armed Forces Journal International (1998): The Indirect Approach:
How US Military Forces Can Avoid the Pitfalls of Future Urban Warfare,
Major General Robert H. Scales, Jr., US Army**

1. General

a. Cities have played a strategic role in military campaigns throughout history. Because of their geographic location, concentration of wealth and power, or symbolic value, cities have been closely associated with strategic objectives in most of history's conflicts. While this basic concept remains true, the city has evolved to become an urban area thus including key infrastructure, critical services, and other military considerations that exist outside the traditional city boundary. Growing urbanization throughout the world raises the possibility of future military operations taking place in urban environments. History and lessons learned demonstrate that the urban environment offers significant operational challenges. The complexity of a specific urban area impacts the planning, decision making, execution, and assessment of operations. Therefore, commanders and their staffs require specific information and analysis to develop an understanding of that environment. This knowledge is necessary to develop the commander's intent and concept of operations (CONOPS) required to attain military objectives while maintaining flexibility to make changes necessary to exploit unforeseen opportunities.

b. This joint publication (JP) focuses on capabilities and tasks that are unique to, or significantly challenged by, urban environments at the operational level. It does not attempt to replace or reiterate doctrine in overlapping areas; instead, it examines the special considerations required when conducting operations in the complex modern urban environment.

c. **Joint urban operations (JUOs)** are joint operations planned and conducted on, or against objectives within, a topographical complex and its adjacent natural terrain, where man-made construction or the density of population are the dominant features. Commanders and their staffs should consider the complex and dynamic interactions and relationships of the population with the physical terrain and infrastructure.

2. Urban Environment

a. **General**

(1) Urban areas present a complex environment for military operations. This complexity is derived from numerous factors such as location, history, economic development, climate, available building materials, the natural terrain on which they are built, the cultures of their inhabitants, and many other factors. These factors also contribute to urban areas varying in size (both infrastructure density and area covered), population density, interconnectedness, and dependence on other urban centers. This complexity makes every urban environment unique. There are many ways to frame an understanding of the factors influencing the urban environment, one of which is to view the urban environment as an **urban triad** consisting of complex man-made physical terrain, a population of significant size and density and varying sociocultural groupings, and an infrastructure.

(a) **A complex man-made physical terrain** is superimposed on existing natural terrain. This physical terrain consists of man-made structures of varying types, sizes, materials, and construction arranged sometimes in an orderly manner and sometimes randomly. It may be modern or built around an ancient core; it may contain towering buildings or none over three stories.

(b) **A population of significant size and density** inhabits, works in, and uses the man-made and natural terrain. Urban areas are frequently defined according to size, from villages of fewer than 3,000 inhabitants to large cities with populations of over 100,000. Large cities vary enormously in size, ranging in population from 100,000 to over 20,000,000 and in area from several to hundreds of square miles. Sociocultural characteristics are the essential focus of population analysis.

(c) **An infrastructure upon which the area depends** also occupies man-made terrain and provides human services and cultural and political structure for the urban area and often beyond, perhaps for the entire nation. An urban area may have a significant influence beyond a city's boundaries. It may influence a region within the nation, the nation itself, or other countries within a geographical region.

(2) This urban triad view establishes a foundational perspective that reveals an interaction between the physical terrain, the population, and the infrastructure of an urban area. This view also reveals the urban area as a complex and **dynamic system**, with unique political, military, economic, social, information, and infrastructure (PMESII) and other components. Each element impacts, constrains, and influences military operations. The physical terrain presents significant challenges to military operations, particularly maneuver and communications. Infrastructure serves as the essential enabler for economic, information, and social systems, which create varying limitations on military operations if interrupted. While all three elements of the urban triad are important, it is the impact of military operations on the urban population, and vice versa, that fundamentally distinguishes operations in urban environments from operations in other environments.

(3) Density is an overriding aspect of the urban environment: density of structures, density of people, and density of infrastructure. Dense urban geography changes the nature of spatial and temporal relationships and our understanding of them. An overriding aspect of the urban environment is that of **density**—density of structures, density of people, and density of infrastructure. Structural density can create complex social and political

interactions by compressing large numbers of people into a small geographic area. Critical infrastructures (physical, economic, governmental, social, etc.) are in such close proximity and, in most areas, so intertwined that even minor disruptions by military operations can cause significant repercussions. Distances are compressed, often limiting line of sight (LOS) to only a few meters. A very small area can contain a large adversary force and a large number of neutrals, arrayed in three-dimensional depth. For instance, depth may need to be measured in city blocks instead of kilometers. Airspace will consist of layers, with the lower layer perhaps punctured by high-rise buildings or canalized by "urban canyons." The urban tangle, debris, and rubble can slow down all movement to a far slower pace than in other types of terrain. A 10-story building may take up the same linear space on a two-dimensional map as a small field, but the building has eleven times the actual defensible space—10 floors plus the roof and any associated subterranean structures. Volume, not area, is the more pertinent spatial measure of the urban environment. Buildings can block or reduce communications capabilities, resulting in the isolation of a unit. Man-made terrain features can also easily mask other man-made features. Urban areas also tend to have higher densities in a temporal sense; that of more activities to unit time. This form of density, one less often recognized, directly influences intelligence gathering as well as other operations. This may affect both the types and number of resources that may be required to conduct a JUO.

b. **An urban area is dynamic—in a constant state of motion.** Understanding the urban environment requires continuous study and analysis as it is complex, dynamic, and perpetually evolving. To understand a particular urban area, it is necessary to comprehend the underlying characteristics, patterns, change dynamics, and its interconnectedness with the surrounding area.

See Chapter II, "Understanding the Urban Operational Environment," for a more detailed description of the operational environment in urban areas.

3. **Characteristics of Joint Operations in Urban Environments**

a. **Historical Background.** Military thinkers and planners have long been aware of the pitfalls of fighting in urban areas. As early as circa 500 B.C., Sun Tzu advised that "the worst policy is to attack cities," and his advice is echoed in military writings and doctrine to this day. However, despite that sensible advice, wars have been fought in cities repeatedly throughout the centuries, from the sack of Troy to the battles of Fallujah.

(1) Since the beginning of World War II, military operations in urban areas have run the full operational gamut: full-scale ground combat with huge numbers of casualties (Stalingrad, Manila, Seoul); aerial bombing producing hundreds of thousands of casualties in a single day (Dresden and Tokyo); civil war (Beirut, Monrovia); revolution (Managua, Budapest); precision bombing (Baghdad, Belgrade); counterterrorism (Belfast); noncombatant evacuation operations (NEOs) (Monrovia, Beirut); peacekeeping (Sarajevo); foreign humanitarian assistance (FHA) (Mogadishu); nation assistance (Haiti); and others.

URBANIZATION

By the 2030s, five billion of the world's eight billion people will live in cities. Fully two billion of them will inhabit the great urban slums of the Middle East, Africa, and Asia. Many large urban environments will lie along the coast or in littoral environments. With so much of the world's population crammed into dense urban areas and their immediate surroundings, future joint force commanders will be unable to evade operations in urban terrain. The world's cities, with their teeming populations and slums, will be places of immense confusion and complexity, physically as well as culturally. They will also provide prime locations for diseases and the population density for pandemics to spread.

The current demographic trends and population shifts around the globe underline the increasing importance of cities. The urban landscape is steadily growing in complexity, while its streets and slums are filled with a youthful population that has few connections to their elders. The urban environment is subject to water scarcity, increasing pollution, soaring food and living costs, and labor markets in which workers have little leverage or bargaining power. Such a volatile mixture is a recipe for trouble.

There is no modern precedent for major cities collapsing, even in the Eighteenth and Nineteenth Centuries, when the first such cities appeared. Cities under enormous stress, such as Beirut in the 1980s and Sarajevo in the 1990s, nevertheless managed to survive with only brief interruptions of food imports and basic services. The effectiveness of pre-existing infrastructure may be tested as never before under the stress of massive immigration, energy demand, and food and water shortages in the urban sprawl that is likely to emerge. More than ever before, it will demand the cultural and political knowledge to utilize that infrastructure.

Joint forces will very likely find themselves involved in operations in cities. Such areas will provide adversaries with environments that allow them to hide, mass, and disperse, while using the cover of innocent civilians to mask their operations. They will also be able to exploit the interconnections of urban terrain to launch attacks on infrastructure nodes with cascading political effects. Urban geography will provide enemies with a landscape of dense buildings, an intense information environment, and complexity, all of which ease the conduct of operations. Any urban military operation will require a large number of troops, which could consume manpower at a startling rate. Moreover, operations in urban terrain will confront joint force commanders with a number of conundrums. The very density of buildings and population will inhibit the use of lethal means, given the potential for collateral damage and large numbers of civilian casualties. Such inhibitions could increase US casualties. Additionally, any collateral damage carries with it difficulties in winning the "battle of narratives."

SOURCE: *The Joint Operating Environment,* 2010

(2) Urban battle became particularly common in the 20th century. The control of political, industrial, commercial, transportation, and communication centers decisively affected the outcome of battles, campaigns, and wars. Technological advances, particularly in aviation, have made it possible to take war to the cities in a more precise manner than in the past with significantly fewer civilian casualties and less collateral damage. Cities themselves have increased in number, size, and strategic importance, resulting in an increase in limited contingency operations. This included a corresponding increase in the operational limitations placed upon military forces conducting these operations.

b. **Modern Joint Operations in Urban Environments.** Figure I-1 provides a general comparison of factors influencing the most common operations in urban environments with those in other environments. Although JUOs may vary greatly in detail, they share a number of common characteristics.

(1) **Cities may reduce the advantages of the technologically superior force.** The physical terrain of some cities may reduce visual LOS as well as the ability to observe fires. It may also inhibit the command and control (C2) processes, some types of communications reliability, in addition to making aviation operations and airspace deconfliction extremely difficult. Moreover, it can decrease the effectiveness of joint fire support. It may also degrade logistics, and reduce ground operations to the level of small unit combat. Additionally, the constraints (a requirement that dictates an action) and restraints (a requirement that prohibits an action) imposed by the need to minimize civilian casualties and preserve infrastructure may further reduce the technological advantage.

(2) **Ground operations can become manpower-intensive.** During phase II (seize the initiative) through phase IV (stabilize) of an operation or campaign (using the notional operation plan phases described in JP 5-0, *Joint Operation Planning*) the joint force requires sufficient ground and other combat forces to clear buildings and control or secure the existing infrastructure and population and to perform other tasks. There will not be a smooth linear transition between phases. This may require some forces to be engaged in combat, while other forces engage in stability operations, each having its specific impact on the number and capability of employed troops. Additionally, as the operation or campaign transitions from phase IV (stabilize) to phase V (enable civil authority), the number and capability of forces will change, often increasing the requirement for ground forces, especially if there is an insurgency or terrorist threat. The structure and duration of this presence will also be influenced by the ability of the host nation's (HN's) security forces and other multinational forces to protect the population and establish a governing structure.

(3) **Ground operations become decentralized.** The dispersal of units into buildings, underground passages, streets, and alleys decentralizes ground operations. This decentralization, combined with the nature of various tasks normally being accomplished by small units, complicates C2, combat identification (CID), information sharing, and target identification.

(4) **Operations are time-consuming.** Nearly all operations in urban areas take significantly longer than originally expected. The prolonged battles for Stalingrad, Aachen in 1944, and Khorramshahr during the Iran-Iraq war (1980-1988) all delayed the attacker

Comparison of Operations in Urban and Other Environments

Aspect	Urban	Desert	Jungle	Mountain
Number of civilians	High	Low	Low	Low
Amount of valuable infrastructure	High	Low	Low	Low
Multidimensional operational environment	Yes	No	Some	Yes
Restrictive rules of engagement	Yes	Some	Some	Some
Detection, observation, engagement ranges	Short	Long	Short	Medium
Avenues of approach	Many	Many	Few	Few
Freedom of vehicular movement and maneuver	Low	High	Low	Medium
Communications functionality	Degraded	Fully Capable	Degraded	Degraded
Logistics requirements	High	High	High	Medium

Figure I-1. Comparison of Operations in Urban and Other Environments

longer than was estimated, resulting in the modification of operational or strategic plans. During the battle for Hue (1968), it took US Marines three weeks of door-to-door fighting to clear a seven-block area.

(5) **Combat operations in urban areas may result in large ratios of civilian to military casualties.**

(6) **Operations conducted in urban areas may have more restrictive operational limitations than operations elsewhere.** The presence of civilians and the need to preserve infrastructure greatly influence operations and help shape the rules of engagement (ROE) and rules for the use of force (RUF). Operations-specific ROE or RUF are often clarified and refined as required by the situation to allow flexibility in accomplishing the mission while limiting civilian collateral damage and friendly casualties. The majority of urban battles since 1967 have had one or more of the following constraints or restraints imposed on the forces engaged: limiting friendly casualties; minimizing civilian casualties and/or collateral damage; or restrictions in the use of ground or air weapons.

(7) **Urban terrain and infrastructure impact weapons employment and munitions effectiveness.** Targets are easily masked by structures. The composition of buildings and surrounding structures changes weapons effects. The layout of the city (streets and building structure) tends to channelize the blast effects of munitions. Historically, some

indirect-fire weapons systems have been used more effectively in a direct fire mode (e.g., artillery), and others used for different purposes (e.g., antitank weapon, used to breach walls or provide openings to buildings). In urban battles since World War II, artillery, antitank weapons, and antiaircraft weapons have proven more valuable in a direct fire role against targets than in their primary roles. Precision munitions can be employed during a JUO to prevent friendly fire, minimize civilian casualties, and limit collateral damage. Consideration should be given to the method of marking of targets within the potentially restrictive urban terrain. The impact of the urban environment on weapons employment makes the inclusion of joint intelligence preparation of the operational environment (JIPOE) and human intelligence (HUMINT) in the planning process that much more critical. The results of JIPOE and HUMINT may minimize the need to employ weapons or may lead to more accurate targeting, thereby reducing collateral damage.

(8) **Urban areas provide advantages to defenders.** Urban areas reduce the advantages in numbers and equipment of attacking forces. In both combat and limited contingency operations, urban areas provide benefits to those who could use the civilian population and infrastructure to their advantage. Conversely, isolation of an urban defender affords the attacker a significant, often decisive advantage.

(9) **Urban areas generally have a concentration of media outlets representing all types of format (print, broadcast, Internet) with a variety of allegiances.** This concentration makes it easy to cover operations without relying on outside assistance, including that of the US military. Real-time reporting from the urban battlefield and subsequent public and political reaction can limit the options available to commanders particularly with regard to use of force. Media hostile to the US can misrepresent or lie about the results of military operations to further their agenda. Additionally, mass information dissemination is no longer the sole purview of commercial media. Any individual observing military operations with access to the Internet can post information and images that have the potential to reach millions of people, influencing their perceptions about military operations. This is particularly true in urban environments where operations are often conducted under the observation of the citizenry. The on-scene commander has the responsibility to understand the media situation and ensure that it is addressed in the planning process and that troops are prepared for these eventualities.

(10) **Despite its many disadvantages, ground combat may be the most effective and efficient way for a commander to accomplish operational or strategic objectives.** Urban ground operations, although infantry intensive, require effective combined arms integration at all levels. Offensive operations with the purpose of securing an urban area and destroying the adversary defending it, or defensive operations with the objective to deny the urban area to the adversary, are difficult and costly. All those aspects of urban ground combat that have historically extracted a terrible price on attacker, defender, and civilian alike remain present today, multiplied by the increased size and complexity of urban areas and increase in the number of inhabitants. Even if ground combat operations are necessary, appropriate shaping of the operational environment, identification of the center of gravity (COG), and precise application of force may prevent full-scale urban combat. The joint force commander (JFC) should consider forces and functions in unusual combinations and relations when conducting JUOs, befitting the nature of the urban operational environment.

(11) **The requirements to protect and aid civilians and to preserve and restore infrastructure create competing demands with tasks requiring defeat of the adversary.** Increased use of fires may kill more of the foe and preserve friendly force lives, but it may also be counterproductive because of the extent of collateral damage and civilian casualties caused. These issues must be continually assessed in order to capitalize on opportunities, limit risk, comply with the law of war, and adjust operations accordingly.

(12) **The presence and involvement of organizations from other United States Government (USG) departments and agencies, nongovernmental organizations (NGOs), intergovernmental organizations (IGOs), and the private sector will impact military operations.**

(13) **Intelligence support requirements are different and more demanding in urban areas.** An analysis of the threat is essential as is detailed intelligence and information on the physical terrain and infrastructure characteristics of the urban environment. This intelligence will be developed during the JIPOE process. Furthermore, input regarding the population—civilian leaders, civilian groups, and the relationships between these and other non-threat-related factors—will be crucial to ultimate operational success. Developing the necessary intelligence products to support operations in an urban environment is a cross-functional effort. It is driven by the primary theater intelligence production element, the joint intelligence operations center, but includes joint task force (JTF) directorates, Department of Defense (DOD), and other government and nongovernment agencies.

(14) **Cities are heterogeneous; the challenges and solutions in one area of a city may be greatly different from those in other areas of the city.**

(15) **JUOs are not conducted in isolation from the city's rural and suburban surroundings.** Rural areas may allow enemy forces or insurgents the opportunity to store weapon caches and threaten lines of communications (LOCs). Forces must be prepared to conduct operations in both urban and rural areas simultaneously. Commanders should not become overly focused on an urban area within a larger joint operations area (JOA). Threats and other influences can come from elsewhere. The area of interest (AOI) therefore extends well beyond an urban area and its immediate environs.

(16) **The requirement for the relative emphasis among offense, defense, and stability operations may vary unpredictably.** Cities tend to increase the density among the multiple tasks inherent in providing support, maintaining stability, and waging combat.

(17) **The ability to detect deviations from "normal" urban patterns is an invaluable capability.** Understanding what "normal" is in an urban area inherently allows the joint force to detect what is otherwise. Understanding urban patterns supports assessment and has value at the strategic, operational, and tactical levels. Understanding urban patterns is a time-consuming effort and requires patience, attention, and the focused observation skills of the joint force.

(18) **Forces conducting JUOs may face increased exposure to communicable diseases and toxic industrial materials (TIMs) (e.g., toxic industrial chemicals, toxic**

industrial biologicals, and toxic industrial radiologicals) and/or attacks with actual weapons of mass destruction (WMD). Risks and consequences of these threats will vary based on the unique environment of a particular city (e.g., weather, density, sanitation). In some instances, the urban environment might assist in mitigating the effects of such incidents. The environment may also exacerbate the effects of agents, which may stagnate in closed areas or be communicated to combatants through contact with civilians.

(19) **Forces will likely face increased exposure to potential isolating incidents.** The risks of overreacting in the urban environment include additional opportunities for the enemy to take hostage friendly or multinational personnel for monetary, ideological, psychological, and/or propaganda purposes.

4. Air Operations Considerations

a. Air operations must adapt to the unique urban environment. The urban environment includes challenges such as CID, propensity for collateral damage, preservation of infrastructure, restrictive ROE, LOS obstructions (to include targeting and communications), and freedom of maneuver. Although C2 of air power does not change in the urban environment, tactics, techniques, and procedures (TTP) may be vastly different from those employed on the open battlefield. Planners need to consider that urban ground operations will be largely decentralized and coordination will be more time-consuming. For example, large munitions may be traded for increased loiter time in fuel as smaller precise weapons are more desirable for employment to reduce collateral damage in cities or towns. Public affairs (PA) planners should be involved early in the process to mitigate negative events. Finally, air operations in an urban environment involve significant law of war considerations. In particular, commanders, planners, and aircrew, after consultation with their staff judge advocate (SJA), determine whether the operation satisfies the law of war, the ROE or RUF, and other considerations.

b. Close air support (CAS) may be difficult when supporting house-to-house ground fighting, where locating and identifying friendly positions may prove highly demanding, and friendly forces are often in closer proximity to the enemy than in open terrain. Techniques such as developing gridded reference graphics may prove useful in identifying enemy and friendly positions. Aircrew and fires personnel should give extra attention to the axis of attack and target designation. Interference from buildings may hamper communications between ground forces and aircraft, complicating CAS employment. Ground forces may have difficulty marking targets for CAS aircraft in urban terrain, while the "bird's eye view" of aircraft may help mitigate ground forces' LOS limitations. Precise and low collateral damage ordnance has proven particularly effective in urban operations. Aircraft with long on-station times and high-fidelity sensors have been useful in the urban environment, where target sets are often in close proximity to civilians and friendly forces.

5. Conditions for Urban Engagement

a. When necessary to accomplish strategic or operational objectives, the JFC designs, plans, and executes operations in urban areas with due consideration of the strategic environment as well as existing and potential operational limitations.

b. Operations in urban areas may occur within the context of a campaign or major operation. These operations may take place entirely within a city or may include multiple urban areas and may be influenced by interconnected surrounding areas. The JFC will determine whether or not operating in an urban environment is essential for the conduct of the campaign or major operation and, if so, where and when to conduct JUOs. The following strategic and operational considerations and requirements may determine whether JUOs are necessary:

(1) An urban area may have infrastructure and/or capabilities that have strategic or operational value, and the military necessity of destroying, degrading, denying, neutralizing, exploiting, or seizing these critical features must be carefully weighed against not only the impact on the populace, but also the costs and risks to the operation.

(2) It may be necessary to isolate an adversary in an urban area to facilitate a larger operation or campaign in another location.

(3) The geographical location of an urban area may dominate a region or avenue of approach.

(4) The political and cultural significance of the urban area may be such that it is itself a strategic or operational COG or has a relationship to the designated COG.

c. When faced with the prospect of operating in urban areas, the JFC should carefully consider whether or not the means are available to conduct the operation successfully considering the demands of the urban environment. In addition to the questions outlined in Figure I-2, the JFC should consider force strength, force types, required munitions and equipment, potential casualties, potential personnel recovery (PR) incident risks, the effects of time and momentum, the potential for collateral damage, the prospects of escalation, and alternative courses of action (COAs). These alternatives might include seizure or construction of alternate facilities (such as port or airfield) or bypassing and isolating the urban area rather than entering it.

d. The commander sets the conditions that will lead to the accomplishment of certain tasks. These tasks may include (but are not limited to) isolating the urban area; avoiding template or checklist planning and predictability; developing accurate situational awareness, including knowledge of the population; taking advantage of local expertise; and leading disciplined troops possessing necessary skills gained through realistic urban training and experience.

6. Fundamentals of Operations in Urban Environments

This publication provides a framework on how to operate in an urban environment to defeat adversaries embedded and diffused among the population, without causing catastrophic damage to the functioning of the society. The embedded adversary must not merely be attacked with destructive force, but must be attacked comprehensively. The entire urban environment must be addressed simultaneously and systematically by applying power to disable hostile elements and enable those environmental elements that are essential to the city's functioning. A comprehensive and systematic approach requires a combination of isolating, protective, improving, sustaining, persuasive, destructive, and disruptive actions or capabilities.

The Decision to Conduct Joint Urban Operations

- What is the desired strategic end state?

- Is political, military, economic, social, informational, and infrastructure control of an urban area necessary to attain the desired strategic end state? If yes, what degree of control is required?

- What operational objectives are necessary in order to attain the level of desired political, military, economic, social, informational, and infrastructure control of an urban area?

- Can the joint force accomplish the necessary operational objectives with the means and time available?

- Are the anticipated consequences and costs of accomplishing the necessary operational objectives justified by the importance of the desired strategic end state?

Figure I-2. The Decision to Conduct Joint Urban Operations

a. **Conduct a systemic assessment.** The basis for planning and executing is an understanding of the urban area as a complex dynamic environment with various structures, processes, and functions, which will be disrupted by military operations but which are essential to the continued viability of the area.

b. **Integrate all actions within the context of an overarching major operation or campaign.** Combine the various isolating, protective, improving, sustaining, persuasive, destructive, and disruptive actions, military and nonmilitary, into a cohesive, mutually reinforcing whole.

c. **Learn and adapt.** Since an urban environment is complex, and since it is ever evolving, design operations with a flexibility to adjust timing, forces, and other aspects to seize opportunities and react to unforeseen challenges.

d. **Selectively isolate key portions of the urban environment.** Control the influx into the urban environment of people, materiel, and information that could help support the adversary.

e. **Apply highly discriminate, destructive, or disabling force to disrupt an adversary's ability to pursue its objectives.** Actively locate and attack enemy elements while minimizing impact on other elements of the urban environment.

f. **Establish and extend control and protection of urban sectors and subsystems.** Create a secure environment that allows enabling actions to occur and may help gain the allegiance of the population, while at the same time denying the adversary access to segments of the population and other key resources.

g. **Persuade municipal governments, groups, and population segments to cooperate with joint force operations.** Influence indigenous perceptions and attitudes through the military's communication synchronization efforts in accordance with strategic guidance.

h. **Provide essential support into the urban environment to sustain it during the ordeal of combat operations to improve its ability to survive.**

i. **Support improvements to urban institutions and infrastructure.** Support the restoration or creation of essential subsystems as a means to enable the urban environment to better sustain itself.

CHAPTER II
UNDERSTANDING THE URBAN OPERATIONAL ENVIRONMENT

"If you don't understand the cultures you are involved in; who makes decisions in these societies; how their infrastructure is designed; the uniqueness in their values and in their taboos—you aren't going to be successful."

George C. Wilson
A Lesson in Peacekeeping, *Air Force Times*, 11 March 1996

1. General

a. **Introduction.** Operational environment is defined as a composite of the conditions, circumstances, and influences that affect the employment of capabilities and bear on the decisions of the commander. It encompasses physical areas and factors (of the air, land, maritime, and space domains) and the information environment (which includes cyberspace). Included within these are the adversary, friendly, and neutral systems that are relevant to a specific joint operation. By understanding key aspects of the operational environment through a systems perspective, the JFC and joint planners can then choose dynamic ways to achieve operational objectives. It is important to note, the complexity of the urban environment increases the possibility and incidence of undesired effects or unforeseen consequences from any military operation.

b. **Precepts for JUOs**

(1) **Cities are built to sustain human life.** Of all facts about cities, this one is the most significant and forms the foundation of all the other precepts.

(2) **Cities are not natural entities,** in that they do not arise without human intervention upon a given natural environment. Since cities arise for the reasons of those who build them, the shape, design, and functions of a city are well within the reach of understanding. As such, cities may be analyzed on a military as well as any other basis. A military analysis of a city must be founded upon information that is pertinent to one's mission or tasks, and a significant part of this analysis will derive from the character of the city itself.

(3) **Cities do not exist in a vacuum.** Every city exists within a physical network of other cities, towns, villages, suburbs, or exurbs. Every one of these lesser aggregations defines itself at least partly by reference to the greater city, just as the greater city defines itself, at least partly, by reference to its surroundings. The existence of greater and lesser urban zones within mutually supporting distance should alert any military analyst or planner to how forces might be disposed.

(4) **Cities should not be regarded as inert.** Malfunction of public systems, catastrophes, natural disasters, civic disorder, crime, riot, insurrection, or invasion and occupation—all these impact the relationship among physical terrain, population, and infrastructure.

(5) At a certain point in their growth, **cities attain a level of complexity that is the product of human and physical synergy.** That point occurs when some degree of higher management is required. Urban complexity, improperly managed, can act as a dysfunctional force in a city. The military significance of urban complexity is that its dysfunctional tendency can be accelerated. It is not only that there are more moving parts, it is that those parts are moving differently.

(6) The inherent social and material order of a city may be described as **urban cohesion.** Urban cohesion manifests itself continuously and practically by acting as a counterbalance to urban complexity. In essence, urban cohesion is attained when an individual subordinates oneself to a larger group in order to benefit less immediately but more reliably. Urban organization is made possible by widespread social agreement.

(7) **Cities tend to persist.** Cities exhibit adaptive capacities that often strain credulity. Toward the end of the latest battle of Grozny (1999-2000), Russian authorities estimated that upwards of 35,000 civilians remained in a city where no buildings escaped serious damage, and no regular services existed, and movement was possible only at night. Cities are highly adaptive entities.

c. **The nature of the urban operational environment is adaptive.** The urban environment is made up of adaptive systems with a wide range of structures, processes, and functions that have evolved to sustain concentrated human societies in confined space. These structures are all the various familial, tribal, professional, commercial, governmental, social, religious, educational, and media institutions that typify urban society. The processes include all the various official and unofficial social, criminal, economic, governmental, informational, and cultural interactions that take place within the ebb and flow of urban life. Functionally, the urban environment consists of governance, cultural center, manufacturing center, services, a source of jobs, and a marketplace for goods and services. Some of these structures, processes, and functions are fundamental to the functioning of the urban system, providing for basic human needs. These structures, processes, and functions may be generically common to all urban environments, but each urban environment is unique in its specifics. Combat changes urban environments, often significantly and generally for the worse. The essential quality of urban areas by this view is not merely the presence of people, but the presence of intense societal interaction (although not necessarily interactions that are functioning smoothly).

d. **Cohesion**

(1) Urban cohesion has often figured importantly in war and conflict. Armed forces throughout history have struggled against cities' power to resist, to withstand sieges lasting months or years, or to absorb the punishment of entire armies fighting within their precincts.

(2) Cities are normally designed and constructed to function in a peacetime environment. Once established, cities operate at a pace and rhythm unique to themselves, depending on the vitality of their social and material cohesion. A city's infrastructure, common systems, and functioning can be tested by natural disasters, industrial disasters,

GROZNY—THE OPERATIONAL ENVIRONMENT

Near the end of 1994, Russia's Yeltsin Administration, faced with the continuing dissolution of the Soviet empire, committed military forces to restore the Russian Federation's authority throughout the Caucasus region. The Russians originally thought the operation would be a simple demonstration of force in the capital city of Grozny that would rapidly culminate with the collapse of the "rebel" government. This show of force quickly evolved into a military campaign that eventually ended in total failure. Russian commanders may well have avoided this failure, however, had they correctly understood and shaped the battlespace within their theater of operations. Instead, they believed the erroneous assumptions generated at the strategic level and subsequently directed a woefully inadequate effort to understand the battlespace in all its complexity. This disregard for intelligence adversely affected virtually every other warfighting function at the operational level. On the other hand, the Chechen rebels made extensive use of their familiarity with the region and their own first-hand knowledge of the strengths and weaknesses of the Russian Army to the fullest advantage.

SOURCE: Timothy L. Thomas, The Battle of Grozny: Deadly Classroom for Urban Combat, *Parameters,* Summer 1999

civil disorder, military conflict, or outright war. Though persistent, urban systems are dramatically affected, whether intentionally or not, through military and other action.

e. **Threat.** The types of threat present in a particular urban area will vary. The threat may consist of a conventional hostile military force, an unconventional militia or guerilla force (such as those found in Beirut or Mogadishu), terrorists, criminal organizations or gangs, an opposing political group, or a catastrophic or disruptive threat such as a force of nature, hunger, or disease. In fact, it is increasingly typical to have multiple threats appearing simultaneously in the operational area. Friendly forces conducting JUOs may encounter these threats in isolation, but the nature of urban areas makes it increasingly likely that these threats will be found in combination. The complexity of the operational environment creates the ability for adversaries to become indistinguishable from the rest of the population. Military operations may encounter hunger and disease in the civilian population and sometimes hunger and disease are incidental to military operations; natural disasters may produce enough instability to encourage action by guerrillas or militia groups; destruction of infrastructure may lead to increased criminal activity. In any case, the existing and potential threats must overlay the characteristics of the urban area in the commander's thinking concerning the urban operational environment.

f. **Understanding the Operational Environment.** Understanding this operational environment requires a holistic view that extends beyond the adversary's military forces and other combat capabilities within the operational area. This understanding is achieved through the JIPOE process.

See JP 2-01.3, Joint Intelligence Preparation of the Operational Environment, *for more information on the development of a systems perspective as part of the JIPOE process.*

2. Political

The political system describes a structure in which economic interests, political actors, and civic organizations interact to make policy decisions. At the heart of this structure is the delineation of the civil authority known to the population. Unique to JUOs is the requirement to influence political/civil institutions in order to shape outcomes to meet the USG's desired end state. In conjunction with other USG entities, the JFC needs to plan for what elements, to what degree, and to what standards, the JFC will shape the political landscape in accordance with achieving US goals.

3. Economic

a. The economic system describes a structure that provides basic needs and improves the quality of life for the population. Processes within this system are designed to meet the basic needs of the population for health, safety, and economic success.

b. Providing economic assistance in a JUO is a difficult and complicated task that requires coordination and synchronization throughout the economic area of influence. JFCs should set realistic objectives, expect slow progress and setbacks, and prepare their forces for the same. Because incomes have often fallen sharply during the conflict, "normal" living conditions or levels of service are often impossible to define. It is not the job of the military to restore public services or incomes to prewar or other desired levels; that is the job of the citizens of the HN themselves. Depending on the state of the economy, doing so may take considerable time. It is, however, part of the mission of personnel engaged in joint operations to help create the security conditions that can make growth and development possible.

4. Special Social and Cultural Considerations for Urban Areas

a. The social variable describes societies within an operational environment. A society is a population whose members are subject to the same political authority, occupy a common territory, have a common culture, and share a sense of identity. **The commander should keep in mind the overall objectives regarding the civilian populace: to minimize civilian interference with military operations, minimize mission impact on the population, and observe the necessary legal, moral, and humanitarian obligations toward civilians.** Failure in any case may adversely influence the achievement of strategic and operational objectives. However, depending on the mission, these objectives could be negative and too simplistic. Commanders should view civilians as sources of information, components of post-combat success during rebuilding, and, perhaps, those to whom the city will ultimately be turned over.

b. There are several reasons why urban populations complicate, disrupt, and even threaten the success of operations and their attendant intelligence support functions. Some examples include:

(1) Urban populations are composed of many groups and subgroups that may not cooperate with each other or with military forces.

(2) Each group has its own needs, interests, intentions, and capabilities.

(3) Relationships that exist among groups play critical roles in operations.

(4) Cultural differences typically strain relations between the friendly force and the resident population if not understood and appreciated.

(5) People going about their daily routines can unwittingly hamper friendly objectives.

(6) The resident population has survival and living needs that cannot be ignored.

(7) Urban population groups and subgroups increase the number of elements to be identified and assessed as potential threats to the friendly force. They also increase the number of potential groups able to assist the friendly force.

(8) The presence of civilians can escalate tactical actions to episodes of strategic importance.

(9) Tactical forces often adopt an adversarial mentality toward the population that might create gaps in intelligence and barriers to complete analysis.

c. **Human Environment.** Information about the physical security, cultural narratives, economic security, ideology and belief systems, authority figures, and organizations relevant to major social groups in the area under study comprises the human environment. This information may come from open source, unclassified collection and is referenced geospatially, relationally, and temporally to enable the creation of various maps or views of the human dynamics in areas where the joint force has committed resources. Information on social groups and their interests, beliefs, leaders, and the drivers of individual and group behavior is needed to conduct effective operations in urban environments.

(1) The concentration of people has its own demographic characteristics: population density, neighborhoods and their make-up, ethnicity, race, age, daily movement in and around the city, and other considerations based on the nature and behavior of the populace. Other sociocultural characteristics may include religion, political leanings and activity, economics, clan or tribal affiliation, criminal organizations and activities, and class divisions. The population in an urban environment must be considered as a distinct and critical aspect of the commander's assessment. The human dimension is the very essence of the urban environment. Understanding local cultural, political, social, economic, and religious factors is crucial to successful JUOs and becomes central to mission success.

(2) It is important to understand that urban populations are extremely heterogeneous. The overall population is composed of several groups, each with its own

interests. Relationships between groups might be congenial, hostile, or dependent. Understanding this diversity and complexity requires a significant amount of mental effort and flexibility.

(a) The cultural tendencies of urban residents might be very different from what friendly forces are accustomed to. Food, habits, living conditions, laws, religious customs, and beliefs may initially distance a warfighter from the city's residents. The differences must be appreciated by the friendly force in order to achieve and maintain legitimacy within a foreign operational area.

(b) Cultural differences can also affect tactical efforts. In Mogadishu, for instance, groups of civilians protected Somali gunmen by using their own bodies as cover. This unfamiliar tactic created a dilemma for soldiers constrained by the ROE and the law of war. It is important to recognize, however, that not all sectors of the population, including those that at first glance may appear threatening, necessarily work against the friendly force. Individuals and groups of all backgrounds can be co-opted or influenced by the friendly force to serve a friendly or benign objective.

(c) The abundant population groups and subgroups inherent to cities make threat identification difficult. Unlike more traditional operations on open terrain, where merely spotting an unknown entity would assist in deciphering friend from foe, urban areas are packed with individuals and groups that might have the capabilities, interests, or intentions that can threaten a unit's mission. An analyst may not be able to distinguish urban friend from foe just by simple observation. Knowing what groups exist within the operational area and understanding the interests and intentions of each can help in planning operations that, per the commander's intent, exploit all capabilities and opportunities to accomplish military objectives and support other agencies or organizations in attaining the desired end state.

d. **Culture.** Cultural understanding is a key to success in every aspect of joint operations conducted in urban environments. An urban environment acts like a cultural centrifuge on complex operations. The velocity of events is unforgiving, the pressure becomes unrelenting, and there is a constant threat of separation from the people.

e. **Religion.** In addition to the commonly understood military limitations associated with religious infrastructure (e.g., churches, mosques, temples, shrines) the religious beliefs and practices of a population play a central role in the culture of a society and thus impact operations in urban environments. Considerations may include but are not limited to geographic or regional patterns of religious affiliation; past and present religious conflicts among population groups; religious peculiarities and sensitivities; and relationship of religion to other sources of social affiliation (e.g., ethnicity, economic class, political ideology, family, clans, and tribes). Cities may contain religious shrines and significant religious structures.

f. **Criminal Activity.** The density of population and complex physical terrain allow criminals to blend into the population. Some discount organized criminal groups as a national security or military threat. However, a band of criminals without any political ideology could use the same methods for profit and cause significant disruptions, such as through kidnappings or hostage taking. Sometimes these syndicates may have better resources than insurgents.

(1) Within a city, many factors including squalor, decay, and unemployment are conducive to the recruitment of youth into criminal organizations.

(2) The percentage of a population that involves itself in organized criminal behavior need not be great to present a threat to stability. A criminal group that can control one district of a 10-million plus megacity has more power than most rural insurgents could gain over 20 years of operations. Such power will need to be addressed by any intervening force.

g. **Social Trends**

(1) Urbanization has significant environmental consequences. Shortages of shelter, water, food, and poor sanitization in a densely populated urban environment will inherently cause more casualties than more sparsely populated rural communities. Additionally, the dense population also will allow for rapid transmission of diseases.

(2) Poor urban areas can have unique characteristics and exhibit many special problems, including unachievable resource requirements, significant pollution, and social stresses caused by high population densities. They are also breeding grounds for extreme political and terrorist movements, and they present enormous problems to policing and maintaining civil order.

5. Information Considerations for Urban Areas

a. Information is the pervasive backdrop of the urban environment. It is continuously changing and requires that plans and operational decisions be based on this knowledge and on the results of constant monitoring, assessment, and analysis.

b. In urban settings, the density of population includes a density of media of all types, whose reporting may be friendly, neutral, or opposed to US interests.

c. Informational nodes may include but are not limited to newspapers, television networks, radio stations, computer networks, information technology centers, and postal facilities. The information environment should be examined in the context of global interconnectivity, the national level, and the local level.

For additional information regarding information operations (IO) planning considerations, see JP 3-13, Information Operations.

6. Infrastructure Considerations for Urban Areas

a. The total functioning of an urban area is supported by infrastructure which is itself composed of systems. Each component of infrastructure affects the population, the normal operation of the city, and the nature and long-term success of JUOs. Commanders and their staffs should understand the functions and interrelationships of these systems in order to achieve success.

b. In urban areas, buildings and people are interconnected with phone lines, roadways, sidewalks, electrical wires, drainage pipes, and gas mains, the layout of which often cannot be easily surmised. These connections pose dilemmas for C2, the health and welfare of a unit and the civilian population, logistics, and other aspects of an operation.

c. Urban areas will contain varying degrees of **engineered features as part of their infrastructure.** Variations on the infrastructure will be influenced by the social, cultural, economic, political, and historical composition of the city. In general, cities are built to meet the requirements of the day. Urban planners, architects, civil engineers, and other experts can provide critical insight into the ways in which an urban area operates that can influence the development of a CONOPS. The knowledge supports the attainment of military objectives while preserving critical functionality and minimizing the need for certain stability and reconstruction efforts. While civil affairs (CA), engineer, and other military personnel have some of the skill sets required to accomplish this, the JFC relies on involving experts from the Department of State (DOS) and other USG departments and agencies, displaced and expatriated local officials, civil engineers, and others in a unified assessment and planning effort. The JFC must be able to understand the city from a military point of view–quite a different view from that taken by a resident or even an urbanologist. Seen as a military problem, an elevated expressway curving through a central urban core district is a problem different in kind from the one considered by the planner who designed it. In short, the commander must be prepared to "read" the city. A commander's knowledge about cities in general, particularly how structures relate to city functions, and how functions change under different circumstances, is essential.

d. This infrastructure may include a transportation network, utilities, government buildings, hospitals, schools, food processing and distribution centers, and communications facilities. The infrastructure may be relatively simple or it may be highly complex and sophisticated. For example, transportation infrastructure in one city may be a simple network of streets; in another city, it may consist of sophisticated port facilities, rail networks, airports, large highways, subways, bus system, taxis, and other modes of public transportation. In the latter case, such a city may be the transportation hub for the region in which it is located—if not the entire nation.

e. Disrupted public utilities can create significant obstacles to maneuver, communications, and the use of firepower. Broken water hydrants can deplete a municipality's water resources. Phone and electrical lines restrict helicopter airspace. The capability of utilities to affect many regions of the city gives them the potential to be used as weapons or as weapons platforms. For instance, if the water flow into a city can be controlled, an adversary can intentionally limit that flow and create an urgent need that a joint force must address. This manipulation of the water supply serves as a potentially lethal weapon (people can become dehydrated or overheated) as well as a weapon of influence (fear of having an adversary control a critical need). As a weapon's platform, this same water supply can be tainted with a biological agent that can infect anyone who drinks it, creating disease of epidemic proportions as well as considerable terror in the population.

f. In addition to the physical infrastructure of power plants, transportation networks, and the like, cities also have a **service infrastructure:** police, fire, and other government services; food and water availability and distribution; medical services; fuel and electricity; sanitation; the news media and information flow; education; and others. This sort of infrastructure may be quite sophisticated and an integral part of the city's life, it may be virtually nonexistent, or it may exist in a state of ineffectiveness.

g. One of the most overlooked aspects of infrastructure that may impact operations is that portion of the electromagnetic spectrum that supports many of the population's needs. Each nation maintains a frequency allocation table, which divides the spectrum into usable and protected allocations to support air traffic control, emergency communications, navigation systems, and a wide variety of essential systems and services. Many of these allocations should be protected even during combat operations because disrupting them may cause more harm to operations than good.

For more information, refer to JP 6-01, Joint Electromagnetic Spectrum Management Operations.

h. **The impact of infrastructure on operations** depends on a number of factors: the unique nature of the urban area; the type of operation; operational objectives; the infrastructure's effectiveness; and friendly ability to disrupt, control, or make use of it. In some cases, infrastructure may primarily support adversary forces. In other cases, it may provide support to both the adversary and the civilian populace or it may only provide support to civilians. The Marine Corps Intelligence Activity (MCIA) 2700-002-03, *Urban Generic Information Requirements Handbook (UGIRH),* addresses the complications created by public works and public infrastructure. The *UGIRH* includes a section devoted to questions about the location, composition, and materials associated with public works. The handbook also lists questions about the significance of infrastructure like utilities and religious centers, which can assist the intelligence analyst in deciphering the key aspects of urban infrastructure that can impact operations.

7. **Other Considerations for Urban Areas**

a. **Physical Factors**

(1) The physical environment includes the geography and man-made structures in the operational area. Urban terrain, both natural and man-made, is the foundation upon which the population and infrastructure of the urban area are superimposed. A single city may incorporate high-rise business or administrative sections, suburbs, shantytowns, industrial areas, extensive parklands or other open areas, waterways, and various patterns of street grids and other transportation infrastructure. City patterns may consist of a central hub surrounded by satellite areas, or they may be linear, a network, or segments. Dominating natural terrain features such as coastlines, rivers, and mountains will influence the pattern. Cities may contain street patterns that are a rectangular grid, radial, concentric, or irregular. Additionally, street names may change as they transition from one neighborhood to another. The city also can be viewed in terms of form and function. A city may consist of a core, surrounded by various commercial ribbons, industrial areas, outlying high-rise areas,

residential areas perhaps including shantytowns, and military areas. Buildings may range from single-story wooden or mud dwellings to high-rise apartments and office buildings, from galvanized metal shops to petrochemical plants. They may be closely packed where land space is at a premium or dispersed over several square miles. The infinite ways in which these features may be combined make it necessary to approach each urban area as a unique problem.

(2) The natural terrain features that lie beneath urban edifices influence unit operations. They dictate where buildings can be constructed and how streets align, thereby influencing a unit's scheme of maneuver. In addition, the slope of roads within urban areas often follows the underlying terrain's natural contours. Thus, terrain features within an urban area are included in the overall terrain analysis of a city.

(3) Understanding the physical characteristics of urban areas requires a different way of thinking about terrain. It requires the comprehension of the multidimensional nature of urban terrain, its general forms and functions, and size. The total size of the surfaces and spaces of an urban area is usually many times that of a similarly sized piece of natural terrain because of the complex blend of horizontal, vertical, interior, exterior, and subterranean forms superimposed on the natural landscape. Like other terrain, urban areas consist of **airspace** and **surface areas**. Additionally, there are man-made **supersurface** and **subsurface** areas. Figure II-1 illustrates the types of physical characteristics found in urban terrain. The following terms are provided as they relate only to ground urban operations:

(a) **Airspace** is the area above the ground usable by aircraft and aerial munitions. In urban areas, airspace is broken up by man-made structures of different heights and densities in addition to the irregularities in natural terrain. This produces an "urban canyon" effect that can adversely impact operations. Urban canyons often cause higher wind speeds with unpredictable wind direction and turbulence that can cause some munitions to miss their targets (increasing risk for both collateral damage and friendly fire) and significantly increase risks for rotary wing operations near the surface.

(b) **Surface areas** include exterior ground-level areas of streets and roads, parks and fields, and any other exterior space. These surface areas follow the natural terrain and are themselves broken up by man-made features.

(c) **Supersurface areas** are the roofs and upper floors of buildings, stadiums, towers, or other structures that can be used for movement, maneuver, observation, firing positions, or other advantage.

(d) **Subsurface areas** are areas below ground level that consist of sewer and drainage systems, subway tunnels, utility corridors, or other subterranean spaces. These areas can be used for cover and concealment, movement, and engagement, but their use requires intimate knowledge of the area.

(e) Equally important are considerations of **exterior and interior space:** what is visible from outside buildings or subsurface areas, and the significant range of people, infrastructure, and activity that occurs unseen in the interior of those structures.

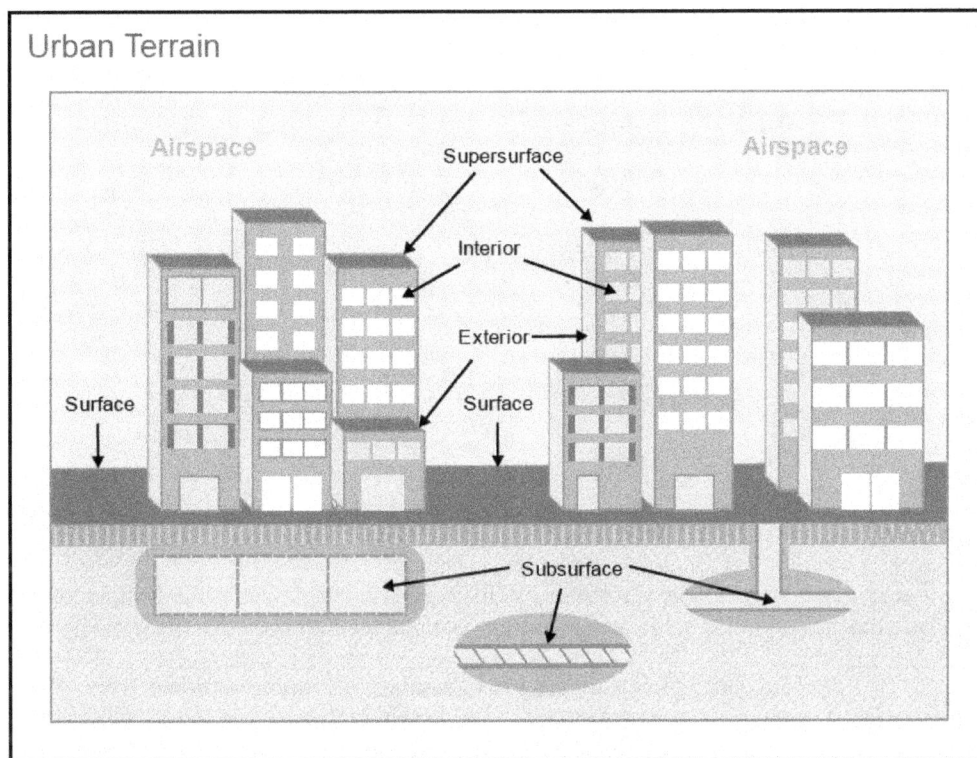

Figure II-1. Urban Terrain

Understanding the full physical nature of an urban area requires a multidimensional approach, with an appropriate awareness of the lateral, horizontal, vertical, and interior and external nature of the city.

(4) Throughout the world, urban areas have similar form and function. In form, urban areas contain like characteristics, readily divisible into distinct sections or areas. Functionally, they tend to be the centers of population, finance, politics, transportation, industry, and culture. While urban areas may be modeled by several different means, Figure II-2 illustrates one example of general forms and internal functions. Some forms and functions may overlap. For example, high-rise buildings are located in core areas as well as in outlying areas and may be used for residential purposes. Visualization in terms of zones enhances understanding of urban patterns and rhythms.

For a more detailed discussion of urban terrain, urban patterns, and urban functional zones, see Field Manual (FM) 3-06, Urban Operations.

(5) FM 2-91.4, *Intelligence Support to Urban Operations,* addresses how to investigate the underlying terrain of a city. It describes how a city's layout affects a unit's ability to operate within it. It also explains how the underlying terrain affects a city's street patterns as well as its distance from other urban areas. Additionally, it discusses how a city's history, ecology, economy, politics, or culture can be influenced by the ground on which it

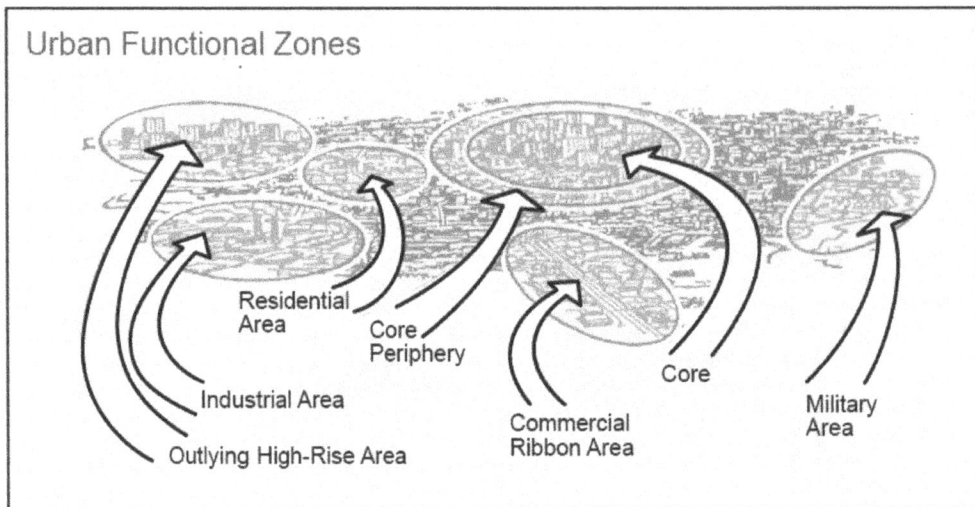

Figure II-2. Urban Functional Zones

sits. For instance, the historical significance of many sites in Israel, such as the Temple Mount, is often more salient to the essence of a conflict than are the buildings that mark them.

(6) Buildings complicate all aspects of military operations in urban areas. Their composition, frontages, size, and window locations affect force positioning and weapons deployment considerations. Angles, displacement, surface reflection, and antenna locations influence communications and intelligence collection. Considerations such as snipers, rubble, booby traps, interfloor movement, and the like are often directly related to urban construction. For instance, buildings increase the numbers of viable approaches for foot soldiers, but limit them for other ground maneuver elements. Snipers, able to hide at any elevation, can become a highly potent weapon for any size force. Rubble is often used for concealment, booby trap locations, or obstacles. The psychological effects of JUOs are also augmented by buildings. Having the adversary able to maneuver and shoot at a multitude of angles and through walls, ceilings, and floors creates psychological and physiological stress in any force.

(a) Buildings also create possible social, cultural, or political dilemmas. Places of worship, government edifices, schools, hospitals, parks, and the like all need to be understood in terms of their significance. Because many cities are peppered with culturally and politically significant buildings, analysts seeking to describe cities face the challenge of accurately identifying and describing them in order to avoid unintended effects.

(b) Generally, under the law of war only those buildings which by their nature, location, purpose, or use make an effective contribution to military action may be targeted. Furthermore, certain types of buildings, particularly hospitals and religious sites, when such buildings or sites are used for their original purposes, have a specific protected status under the law of war that may limit the ability to target them. Additionally, ROE may contain further limitations on targeting. An adversary, however, might not feel bound by the law of war and intentionally target a civilian-use building. Understanding how an adversary might abide by or exploit similar conventions should be part of the planning and analysis process. The complexities associated with targeting in urban terrain underscore the importance of involving judge advocates at all levels in the targeting process.

(c) Buildings can impede intelligence collection efforts. The amount of information that must be collected and assessed regarding structures in urban areas is enormous. Ideally, information about a particular building should include its floor plan in addition to a description of its building materials. Who owns a particular building, who its tenants are, and how it is connected to water and power facilities might also be valuable information. Collecting all of this information, or even knowing which buildings to collect it for, might prove overwhelming. The challenge of assimilating it into an overall analysis of an urban operational area is equally staggering.

(d) Buildings also conceal other relevant operational data. Interior mobility corridors cannot be identified. The condition of the interior can sometimes only be surmised; floor and ceiling stability, the possibility of exposed electrical wires or sewage pipes, and the amount of debris inside a building are indeterminable. The presence of people, both combatant and civilian, is consistently in question. People could be hiding inside buildings, basements, or alleyways waiting to ambush a patrol or waiting for that same patrol to bring them food.

(e) Urban construction has received increased attention in Service doctrinal materials. FM 2-91.4, *Intelligence Support to Urban Operations,* FM 3-06, *Urban Operations,* Army Tactics, Techniques, and Procedures (ATTP) 3-34.80, *Geospatial Engineering,* ATTP 3-06.11, *Combined Arms Operations in Urban Terrain,* and Marine Corps Warfighting Publication (MCWP) 3-35.3, *Military Operations on Urbanized Terrain,* establish procedures for investigating and analyzing the impact of building construction on the employment of forces within an urban area. These manuals and publications describe how to assess the layout of a city, how to analyze the structural characteristics of most buildings, how to deploy and maneuver the appropriate weapons based on these structural characteristics, and how to perform a variety of tactical actions such as clearing a room and breaching walls.

b. **History.** Historic considerations that impact the operational environment may include but are not limited to past wars and military conflicts; territorial claims and disputes; and ethnic, religious, or social strife. Cities may contain areas and structures of historical significance.

c. **Urban Patterns and Rhythms.** Urban areas exhibit patterns that vary both along physical and temporal lines. Discerning these patterns and changes provide insight to social, economic, and other variables. Determining what are normal and abnormal patterns can assist in developing assessment measures. Movement, compressed in space and time, is a normal state of a city, some of whose most important functions entail the sustainment and movement of people, goods, and information. No city can be said to operate at constant velocities, but anyone knows that certain cities have certain rhythms, peculiar to themselves—the most obvious example being their rush hours and early morning cart and truck convoys with goods for the market. These rhythms can be managed—indeed, they are managed all the time—and they can be disrupted as well. Some of these rhythms are critical to maintaining the optimum space-time distributions to which the city has become accustomed. Because these rhythms affect more or less every inhabitant (even if the person is not going anywhere), and because they can be manipulated rather easily, they are militarily significant.

(1) Physical patterns such as market locations and travel routes may provide information regarding security issues and the functioning of other systems. Identification of real or potential transport (of information, people, and material) choke points may provide information of strategic value.

(2) Urban areas have their own unique calendar with daily, weekly, monthly, seasonal, and yearly rhythms. Holidays, festivals, sports, and other events, or their unexpected cancelations may also provide relevant information.

d. **Climate and Weather.** Cities are generally warmer than their surrounding areas; however, at night some portions may cool more quickly than others, so wide temperature variation can occur. Cities may contain heat islands where the daytime temperature may be significantly higher than adjacent areas. Storms and heavy rains may cause flooding and disrupt the infrastructure.

e. **Water.** Urbanization deprives surrounding areas of water. Instead of sinking into the ground, rain is collected, piped to the city, treated, used, and then discarded. In some regions, water levels in local aquifers are declining rapidly because the water that once replenished them now is lost.

CHAPTER III
PLANNING

"Once General Rich Natonski [MajGen Richard F.], the 1st Marine Division Commander, and his staff did their troop-to-task analysis, they asked me for additional forces. So we brought together an operational planning team and worked out a holistic plan to cover ground combat, aviation and combat support, to include operations in Phase IV [after major combat operations], and the forces we'd need to execute the plan. The planning started about a month out..."

Lieutenant General John F. Sattler, US Marine Corps
Commander, Marine Forces Central Command
Second Battle of Fallujah, 2004

1. General

a. Planning for operations that will be conducted in urban environments generally follows the same basic process as planning for operations in other environments. The challenges inherent in operating in an urban area are sufficiently different and complex, requiring commanders and their staffs to give due consideration to the unique requirements of the urban environment. The essential problem is how to operate in an urban environment to defeat adversaries embedded and diffused within populated urban areas without causing catastrophic damage to the existing, functioning society.

b. Operations in urban areas should not be contemplated without an awareness of the characteristics of the area and the lessons derived from past operations.

c. If a major JUO is undertaken as part of a larger campaign, then plans should address the difficult balance, synchronization, and integration between the JUO and the rest of the campaign—including differences in force requirements, tempo of operations, types and quantity of fires and munitions, types and amounts of logistic support, civil-military operations (CMO) requirements, incident response, and many other areas. Whether a JUO is conducted as a major operation during a phase of a campaign or throughout the entire campaign, planning must give appropriate weight to considerations of civilians, infrastructure, the cultural and political situation, demographics, and other urban characteristics that may affect the outcome of the operation.

d. Conducting a JUO is rarely isolated to military forces. JUOs are interactively complex situations involving civilians, infrastructure, and utilities and therefore require integrated solutions synchronized with other significant actors and stakeholders. These actors (e.g., USG officials, IGOs, NGOs, HN governments and security forces) should be imbedded in the planning and operations process.

e. Homeland defense and defense support of civil authorities conducted in an urban environment will be especially demanding in both planning and execution and involve unique legal and policy considerations.

Refer to JP 3-08, Interorganizational Coordination During Joint Operations, *JP 3-27,* Homeland Defense, *and JP 3-28,* Defense Support of Civil Authorities, *for additional information.*

2. The Strategic and Operational Context

a. **General.** The strategic and operational context of operations conducted in urban environments is multifaceted to include the integration of government policies as well as the execution of tactical-level tasks. Events at the tactical level may (because of media coverage, effects on civilians, or other reasons) have significant ramifications at the operational or even strategic levels. Often, the decision whether or not to conduct operations in urban environments is itself a strategic one, taken to control, dominate, or otherwise accomplish objectives in a strategically significant area. Such a decision may also occur at the operational level of war, as part of an operation or campaign plan. As recent history indicates, JUOs will likely have implications at all levels of war.

b. **The Strategic Context**

(1) The decision to conduct a combat operation within an urban area must have a specific tie to the overall end state. Major urban areas are frequently the locations for the airports, harbors, and major road junctions that may be vital for the sustainment of a campaign or operation. From a broader perspective, the JFC must take into account

---

STALINGRAD—THE STRATEGIC CONTEXT

In the summer of 1942, the Germans launched a strategic offensive in southern Russia. The ultimate goal of this offensive was the valuable oil fields of the Caucasus. Capture of the city of Stalingrad would anchor the German defense and simultaneously interdict the critical flow of supplies from the Caspian Sea via the Volga River into central Russia. Stalingrad, by virtue of its name, also had important political and cultural value to the Germans and Soviets.

The opening phases of the German offensive were very successful: German forces—the 6th Army and 4th Panzer Army—entered the outskirts of Stalingrad in late August 1942. By late September, after a month of intense fighting, the Germans possessed 90 percent of the city. The Soviet 62nd Army's defense was reduced to a front only a few hundred meters deep and a couple of kilometers long on the banks of the Volga. The Soviet defense hinged on fortress-like concrete industrial buildings and the fanatical bravery and tenacity of Soviet soldiers and civilians fighting within the remnants of the city. Regiments and divisions fought for a few square blocks or even single factories. Some were swallowed whole by the intense fighting, suffering nearly 100 percent casualties. Beginning in mid-September the Soviet command began looking at how to convert the defense of Stalingrad into an operational opportunity. Throughout October and November, the 62nd Army held on to its toehold in Stalingrad.

While maintaining the defense of Stalingrad, the Soviets secretly began to build up strength on both flanks of the German 6th Army. Powerful German

---

divisions were moved into the city and rotated with German divisions that were largely exhausted by urban combat.

On 19 November, the Soviets launched a counteroffensive that attacked two Romanian Armies with seven Russian Armies. Simultaneously an eighth Russian Army attacked to aid the 62nd Army in further fixing the Germans in Stalingrad. Within five days the Soviet encirclement of the German 6th Army in Stalingrad was complete, due to the German high command's refusal to allow it to withdraw. On 12 December, the German LVII Panzer Corps launched an offensive north to break through to Stalingrad. This offensive made progress until another Soviet offensive on 16 December forced its cancellation. This ended any hope of recovering Stalingrad and the 6th Army. On 31 January 1943, the 6th Army surrendered after sustaining losses of almost two-thirds of its strength. The Soviets took over 100,000 prisoners.

Numerous lessons emerge from the successful defense of Stalingrad, but foremost among them are the strategic and operational ramifications of the battle. The entanglement of the German forces at Stalingrad bought time for the Soviets to mobilize their own forces and launch a powerful counteroffensive. Operationally, the Germans' tactical failure resulted in the destruction of the 6th Army, over 300,000 men. The strategic consequences were even more devastating to the Germans: the drive toward the Caucasus was halted and the oil fields given up; German armies to the south withdrew northward to resist the Soviet offensive; Hitler made major changes in his General Staff and distanced himself from his military leadership; and the confidence of the German Army and the German people was shaken.

SOURCE: William Craig, *Enemy at the Gates: The Battle for Stalingrad,* 1973

aspects of all the instruments of national power when considering undertaking military actions within the urban confines.

(2) Military efforts in urban areas are only effective when integrated into a comprehensive strategy employing all instruments of national power. A successful JUO will not only defeat an adversary, but also will consider the needs of the population and government within the urban structure. Political, social, information, and economic programs are usually more valuable than conventional military operations in addressing the root causes of conflict and undermining an adversary.

c. **The Operational Context**

(1) At the operational level, JFCs plan, conduct, and sustain campaigns and major operations to accomplish strategic objectives within theaters or other operational areas. The requirements and nature of JUOs will make unified action more difficult and complex, and present the JFC with significant challenges in the practice of operational art and operational design.

(2) Because of their physical and human complexity, operations in urban areas tend to be extremely demanding in terms of time, manpower, and certain types of information, equipment, and supplies. Physical and mental drain and the high probability of casualties are realities that must be incorporated into the JFC's plan. The synchronization and integration of time, space, and purpose thus becomes more difficult. Commanders must carefully analyze urban areas in relation to the overall campaign or operation and determine how best to synchronize and integrate operations while preventing urban areas from disrupting the tempo of operations or diverting attention from the accomplishment of higher priority operational objectives.

d. **Mission Analysis.** The primary purpose of **mission analysis** is to understand the problem and purpose of the operation and issue appropriate guidance to drive the rest of the planning process. This involves appreciating each key element of the urban environment as a distinctive system in its own right. Critically, this means appreciating each adversary as a dynamic system as to the basis for defeating it as effectively and efficiently as possible. Different adversaries will require different approaches, as will different elements within the same adversary system. Some could be co-opted, others marginalized or effectively isolated, while some may have to be destroyed physically. Finally, understanding involves analyzing how the adversary interacts with its urban environment; in particular, how each element of the adversary subsists off the systems in its environment, as a means to understanding how to disassociate the two.

(1) Developing a comprehensive understanding will routinely need to be a collaborative effort involving key stakeholders and subject matter experts from various fields, as the type of complex operational problem in a JUO may exceed any one organization's ability to solve, or even comprehend. The requirement for functional knowledge about any given urban environment will place a premium on subject matter experts.

(2) During **mission analysis,** commanders and staffs review their organization and available assets. The complexities and demands of operations in urban environments will always require a complete understanding of the friendly situation. JUOs require unique unit combinations; larger numbers of certain types of assets, units, and equipment; and a specific level/type of unit training. The JFC must accurately determine the capabilities of friendly forces, to include units' proficiency in JUOs and the availability of specialized equipment. Through all phases of the joint operation, the JFC and staff must consider the following questions as a minimum:

(a) What operational objectives must be achieved in urban areas to support the overall plan?

(b) What are the enemy's COGs, critical factors, and decisive points (DPs)?

(c) Must the joint force physically enter the urban area?

(d) What activities and events, and sequencing of these events, are needed to achieve operational objectives?

(e) What resources and application of resources are required to bring about and sustain these activities and events?

(f) What degree, if any, of political and/or military control of the urban area is necessary?

(g) Should the joint force encourage civilians to leave the city, or to remain behind? If the civilians leave, planning should be specific, detailed, and include designated evacuation routes that will not interfere with joint operations, a final destination, and support requirements and plans for their return to the departed areas. If they remain behind, efforts should be made to ensure that they are persuaded to at least remain neutral. Basic emergency services should be planned for those civilians under the JFC's control.

(h) What operational limitations would affect the proposed operation?

(i) Which zones of the city are essential for operational objectives (political centers, military assets, economic centers, social/religious centers, service/transportation nodes-routes-links, information centers, LOCs, historical sites, etc.) and what are the desired results—isolate, neutralize, secure, clear, control, influence, avoid?

(j) What cultural/historical sites must be preserved and how will that impact the operation due to the strategic ramification if damaged or destroyed (e.g., the Mosque, Eiffel Tower, Statue of Liberty)?

(k) What PR considerations exist, including the risk of isolation?

e. Civilians influence the operational limitations faced by the joint force. Their presence places certain constraints and restraints on the JFC.

(1) The joint force may be required to take certain actions toward civilians; these may include protection, control, support, and influence.

(a) **Protection** can take the forms of security against terrorism, law enforcement, removal from combat areas, separation of hostile factions, or other actions.

(b) **Control** includes control of civil unrest and restoration of order, managing civilian movement, and controlling the resources and services on which the populace depends.

(c) **Support** includes provision of basic sustenance, health services, and restoration of services, designed to relieve conditions caused by man-made or natural disaster or other endemic conditions.

(d) **Influence** includes those actions taken by the force to foster support for US objectives by the civilian populace.

(2) **Operational limitations** on the joint force can take the form of restrictions on actions in regard to civilians or restrictions on operations themselves. The law of war

---

CIVILIANS—OPERATION PEACE FOR GALILEE, 1982

Israeli commanders paid a high price for failure to understand the importance of civil affairs. Local Israeli Defense Force (IDF) commanders did not understand the vital importance of civil affairs for ongoing urban combat operations. Thus, civil affairs efforts were ineffectual. Commanders failed to grasp the immediate combat implications or the larger political implications of poor population management. Israeli psychological operations convinced 30,000 noncombatants to flee Tyre and head for beaches outside the city. The subsequent inability of the IDF to provide food, water, clothing, shelter, and sanitation for these people produced predictable consequences. Many tried to return to the city; a process that complicated the northward movement of Israeli troops and the delivery of ordnance on selected targets in Tyre. IDF commanders compounded these oversights by interfering with the efforts of outside relief agencies to aid the displaced population of Tyre lest the Palestine Liberation Organization (PLO) benefit in some way. This second civil affairs failure created an adverse situation that was quickly exploited by PLO psychological warfare specialists. The IDF also failed to educate its troops in dealing with Lebanese civilians. Although the Shi'a Muslim population of southern Lebanon either initially welcomed or was neutral to Israeli presence, it soon became hostile because of the behavior of IDF personnel and other factors.

SOURCE: Marine Corps Intelligence Activity: *Urban Warfare Study: City Case Studies Compilation*

---

identifies those restrictions regarding civilians, and they may be supplemented by specific constraints and restraints provided by the President or Secretary of Defense (SecDef), such as the ROE or the RUF. The presence of large numbers of civilians can also affect mobility, fires, and the employment of obstacles.

f. When planning for operations in urban areas, **the JFC should consider how civilians affect operations and vice versa.** These assessments should be part of the joint operation planning process and are a distinct and critical aspect. In addition, the impact of operations on the civilian populace will likely influence both the commander's ability to conduct operations and the determination of the military end state. Therefore, civilian considerations should form a discrete overall planning area. The human dimension is the very essence of the urban environment. Understanding a wide variety of local cultural, political, social, economic, and religious factors (e.g., racial groups, ethnic groups, religious groups, castes and classes, social grievances, unions, associations, schools, cultural centers, health and welfare facilities, clans, tribes, moral beliefs, social mores, norms of behavior, family structure, and affinity groups) is crucial to successful operations and becomes central to mission success. The human capital of an urban area may be a tremendous resource for the provision of essential services, rebuilding efforts, and reconstituting government systems. The JFC should try to leverage and capitalize on human resources as well as other resources that may be available.

(1) The JFC must consider, as part of the overall determination of operational objectives, the objectives regarding civilians. In doing so, the JFC determines the desired

---

physical and psychological condition of the civilian populace upon termination of hostilities. The commander may then examine civilian considerations through all phases of a joint operation.

(2) Civilians and their actions present operational challenges that influence a commander's decisions and most joint force actions (e.g., military information support operations (MISO), development of ROE, development of HUMINT sources, CMO, assessing humanitarian needs, CA operations, FHA, and population control measures). Prior to high-intensity urban battles, PA and MISO should focus on influencing civilians to leave the prospective operational area or otherwise take actions to minimize their exposure to injury. Where PA and MISO efforts do not prove sufficiently convincing, other enticements need to be considered and offered.

g. When conducting operations in urban environments, several activities regarding the civilian populace must be considered.

(1) **Populace and resources control (PRC)** may be of most critical importance in operations involving combat, but it can also play a key role in noncombat operations. Depending on the location and situation, PRC may be well within the capabilities of the joint force, or it may be an overwhelming task that requires many more resources than the JFC can bring to bear.

(2) **Health support** to civilians is likely to be of vital concern and may require significant action by the joint force.

(3) The joint force may need to provide **logistic support** to civilians and civilian agencies, particularly in the early stages of operations.

(4) **Security issues** relating to civilians include protection of the joint force, security of the civilian population, and security of civilian agencies.

(5) **FHA** operations may require the joint force to plan and conduct activities in support of civilians. Although these support activities are primarily the responsibility of the HN, that nation may be incapable of providing that support, and the joint force may be the only capable support organization for a period of time. It is also highly likely that in any situation where support of large numbers of civilians is required, there will be a strong presence of IGOs and NGOs also trying to relieve suffering and provide for the needs of the civilian populace. The JFC will have to coordinate with those agencies. This coordination may best be accomplished through the actions of the respective directorate and/or the civil-military operations center (CMOC).

h. **Logistic support requirements are different and often more demanding in urban areas.** The complexity of the urban environment places unique demands on sustainment. Operations in urban areas require a significant increase in ammunition expenditure, need for personnel replacements, medical personnel and supplies, casualty evacuation, and food and water. Items most likely to be needed on short notice (such as certain ammunition types, water, and medical supplies) will need to be prepared for quick movement. Vehicles often cannot be evacuated for maintenance. Clothing and equipment are damaged at higher rates. During the 1978 siege of Beirut, Syrian forces required up to 120 truckloads of artillery ammunition per day.

i. Like civilians, infrastructure plays a key role in the planning and execution of any operation conducted in an urban area. The nature of that role can vary depending on the type of operation, the operational objectives, and the phases of an operation. For example, it may be necessary to protect electrical power facilities during foreign internal defense (FID) operations, disrupt them during combat operations, and restore electrical power during the transition phase. **The commander must determine the role and importance of critical infrastructure for each phase of the operation and for the end state. The role and importance falls into two categories: the impact of individual services, facilities, or systems on planned JUOs; and the impact operations may have on critical infrastructure.** In either case, the impact may be direct or indirect—direct, for example, in the disruption of electrical power or the restoration of water services; indirect in the damage to buildings of cultural significance or the improvement of roadways.

j. The JFC and staff analyze the critical infrastructure to determine the relationship between it and friendly and adversary operations and capabilities. This analysis allows the commander to make informed decisions, such as action to be taken in regard to critical infrastructure; requirements for protection, restoration, and joint usage; and estimates of the likelihood and potential effects of collateral damage, both physical and environmental. This analysis takes into account all phases of an operation and includes considerations for air, land, and maritime components. The SWEAT [sewage, water, electricity, academics, trash] model can provide a framework for analysis.

k. **Critical Infrastructure Analysis**

(1) Before a critical infrastructure analysis is conducted, the commander determines what factors make certain facilities important enough to be considered "key." These factors may include such elements as whether and by whom a facility or service is required, the probable effects of its neutralization or use by friendly or adversary forces, and its importance to the civilian population. Planners take these factors and examine all systems and subsystems of the urban infrastructure, both physical and service, in order to identify the key facilities. These systems can generally be grouped as one of the following:

(a) Communications and information.

(b) Transportation and distribution.

(c) Energy.

(d) Economics and commerce.

(e) Administration and human services, which includes law enforcement, health and sanitation services, water distribution, and structures of social, political, religious, or cultural significance.

(f) WMD production facilities and dual-use facilities that could be used to produce WMD.

(2) Critical infrastructure analysis is a combination of intelligence preparation, the targeting process, and staff planning. Its purpose is to examine closely the nature of the infrastructure systems and their components.

(a) Examine each system in terms of its characteristics, organization, and capabilities.

(b) Determine how the system affects the civilian population, how it might support or hinder operations, and what potential effects different operational actions might have.

(c) Break the system down into its components. Consider not only the components, but also the relationships between them as interactions may be just as important as components, and sometimes more so.

(d) Analyze each facility making up each infrastructure system, using the same measures used for the system as a whole.

(e) Recommend COAs for each key component, with short- and long-term potential effects.

(3) The simplified example of a critical infrastructure analysis for the transportation system in Figure III-1 illustrates the procedures involved.

l. **Selection, Protection, Restoration, and Joint Usage**

(1) **Selection.** The initial steps in the critical infrastructure analysis will identify certain infrastructure to be preserved, protected, or to which damage should be minimized. These systems and facilities may be selected for several reasons:

(a) Features of cultural, religious, medical, or other significance whose protection is required under the law of war.

(b) Infrastructure whose destruction would cause hardship for civilians.

(c) Infrastructure which, for strategic or other reasons, is protected by the ROE, and

(d) Infrastructure that the joint force will require for its own use.

(2) **Protection.** The JFC has several methods of protecting selected critical infrastructure. The targeting process should recognize the facilities or structures to be protected and give careful consideration to potential collateral damage resulting from attacks on nearby targets. ROE can include restrictions on actions related to protected sites. In

---

Critical Infrastructure Analysis (Transportation)

1. The urban transportation system may consist of a port, airfields, rivers/canals, a road network, railways, bridges, and subways.

2. An analysis of bridges will look at them collectively and at each bridge by itself.

3. For each individual bridge, the analyst would complete a two-step procedure:

   - Conduct a close examination of the bridge.

     ○ Characteristics: May include length, width, type, structure make-up, number of spans, condition, clearances, and other information.

     ○ Organization: May include obstacle crossed, route designation, condition of bypasses and approaches, condition of banks and support structures, safety and security features, traffic control, and others.

     ○ Capabilities: May consist of maximum load capacity, daily traffic use, effect of weather and climate, and others.

     ○ Role as infrastructure: How the bridge functions in the overall transportation system and its role in support of the civilian populace.

     ○ Use by friendly forces: Whether and how friendly forces might use the bridge in the future.

     ○ Use by adversary forces: How the bridge is or may be used to support adversary forces and actions.

   - Recommend courses of action

     ○ Recommend joint force action toward the bridge and project the effects each course of action may have on the adversary, on friendly forces, on the civilian populace, and on the rest of the urban area's infrastructure.

Figure III-1. Critical Infrastructure Analysis (Transportation)

order to reduce damage when necessary to attack protected sites, alternative methods can be used (e.g., precision guided munitions, weapons restrictions, nonlethal capabilities).

(3) **Restoration**

(a) **In the case of certain critical infrastructure, the JFC will desire to minimize damage on an otherwise legitimate target.** In this case, the objective will be to temporarily disrupt the service that critical infrastructure provides in order to accomplish strategic or operational objectives, but be able to restore that service when desired. **Planning should therefore include an understanding of the functioning of that component of the critical infrastructure system and what may be required in order to repair or restore it.** For example, if the JFC decides to disrupt electrical power to an urban area, planners would

---

require advice from an engineer familiar with the provision of electrical power to an urban area. That engineer would advise planners concerning key parts of the system, feasible ways to disable those parts, and the requirements in time and assets required to restore the system to operation. The JFC can then take the necessary steps to restore usage when appropriate.

(b) Restoration of critical infrastructure is not restricted to the repair of facilities or systems. It can also consist of the restoration of services such as law enforcement, emergency services, or medical services. Restoration of these services may be a lengthy process and must be incorporated in the JFC's CMO planning.

(4) **Joint Usage**

(a) In any ground operations in an urban area, the joint force will use existing infrastructure. This usage may be as simple as driving vehicles on city streets, the appropriation of an entire system such as an airport, or a complex sharing of many infrastructure systems that serve the urban area. Before a decision is made to use existing infrastructure, planners must examine its characteristics, functions, availability, suitability, and the effects of joint use on operational objectives, including the effects on the population.

(b) Most of the information required to plan joint usage will come from the critical infrastructure analysis, particularly data concerning characteristics, capabilities, and functions. From that data and the needs of the joint force, planners must determine the availability and suitability for joint use. When infrastructure is selected for possible joint usage, planners should determine the potential effects joint use would likely have on the civilian populace, local government, and other infrastructure. Planners then determine the impact the availability and suitability of key facilities will have on the accomplishment of operational objectives. Finally, the legal advisor should review any plans for joint force use of infrastructure for adherence to applicable laws and regulations.

m. **Collateral Damage and Environmental Considerations**

(1) Coordination of JUOs through the joint targeting coordination board can significantly reduce collateral and environmental damage. **The objective is to control as carefully as possible the effects of operations on infrastructure and the civilian populace.**

(a) Critical infrastructure analysis can aid in the selection of targets in urban infrastructure to ensure that they meet specific objectives. Target analysis and weaponeering can determine the potential for collateral and environmental damage resulting from attack of a particular target.

(b) In urban concentrations of people and infrastructure, the potential for serious environmental consequences is typically greater than in less populated areas. To accurately predict the environmental damage and its consequences that may occur as a result of attacks, planners require expert advice in the particular areas concerned. For example, an attack on a chemical plant in a predominantly rural area is likely to directly affect fewer people in the near-term than if the plant were in an urban area, but the full extent of environmental damage may not be understood for years. When assessing critical infrastructure that has environmental hazards, careful assessment of not only first-order effects, but also second- and third-order effects must be considered. Subject-matter experts can predict the effects not only on the target area but also in the surrounding areas, to include pollution, spillage, and persistence.

(2) In the end, analysis of potential collateral and environmental damage must be weighed against the importance of the target in achieving operational and strategic objectives. In making that determination, the JFC should examine the short- and long-term operational and strategic consequences that any damage might have on the conduct of operations, friendly forces, the civilian populace, infrastructure, and public perception.

3. Joint Intelligence Preparation of the Operational Environment

JIPOE is the analytical process used by joint intelligence organizations to produce intelligence assessments, estimates, and other intelligence products in support of the JFC's understanding of the operational environment and decision-making process. It is a continuous process that involves four major steps: defining the operational environment; describing the impact of the operational environment; evaluating the adversary; and determining and describing adversary potential COAs, particularly the adversary's most likely COA and the COA most dangerous to friendly forces and mission accomplishment. The process is used to analyze the physical domains (air, land, maritime, and space); the information environment (which includes cyberspace); PMESII systems; and all other relevant aspects of the operational environment, and to determine an adversary's capabilities to operate within these environments. JIPOE products are used by joint force and component and supporting command staffs in preparing their estimates and are also applied during the analysis and selection of friendly COAs.

For additional information, see JP 2-01.3, Joint Intelligence Preparation of the Operational Environment, *and Appendix A, "Joint Intelligence Preparation of the Operational Environment in Urban Areas."*

4. Operational Art and Operational Design

a. **General.** With an understanding of the urban environment and application of operational art, a JFC can successfully conduct a JUO, even in situations where an adversary has been able to use the urban environment to achieve a temporary advantage. **Operational art integrates ends, ways, and means across the levels of war.**

For more detailed discussion of operational art and operational design, see JP 5-0, Joint Operation Planning.

(1) When planning an operation or campaign to deal with adversaries within urban environments, the JFC must go beyond the idea of attacking the embedded adversary. The entire urban environment must be treated comprehensively, applying power to disable hostile elements and enabling those elements that are essential to the city's functioning.

(2) The reality of the urban environment presents a unique set of circumstances and parameters, which will significantly influence the approach to operational art. Commanders

OPERATIONAL ART IN RAMADI

In the past, dealing with complexity was the writ of generals and admirals, usually performed by strategic leaders down to the commander of a theater of operations in charge of a campaign. Today, commanders at much lower levels must master these skills. Consider, for instance, the recent experience of Colonel Sean MacFarland, commander of 1st Brigade, 1st Armored Division. In June 2006, Colonel MacFarland was ordered from Tal Afar in northern Iraq to Ramadi in the west. "I was given very broad guidance," he said. "Fix Ramadi, but don't destroy it. Don't do a Fallujah." He had to determine how to forge relationship with the residents and take the city back from insurgents without launching a general assault. It was his responsibility to share his understanding of his piece of the overall problem with his superiors, not the other way around. He is not the only brigade commander who has used operational art. Some of what the average battalion commander does today is much more like operational art than tactics. Commanders at lower echelons will face ill-structured problems like this where the burden of understanding is squarely on their shoulders alone.

SOURCE: Commander's Appreciation and Campaign Design
US Army, 2008

at all levels must fit the execution of short-term operations into a larger operational design, and this design must link their near-term actions to the end state.

(3) Operational design, as used within the urban context, seeks shared understanding. It seeks to explain the qualitative relationships embedded within the urban environment, including the history, dynamics, propensity, and trends. Nevertheless, it recognizes that complete knowledge is not achievable, and therefore constantly questions the limits of existing knowledge and prevailing public myths or paradigms. JFCs and their staff may have difficulty agreeing on the structure of a specific urban environment, but they must agree on shared starting assumptions and interpretations of the situation and conditions before they can develop proposed solutions. Having shared understanding of the situation is the core of the discussion in Chapter II, "Understanding the Urban Operational Environment." JFCs leverage the following elements of operational design, as described in JP 5-0, *Joint Operation Planning*: termination, military end state, objectives, effects, COG, DPs, lines of operation (LOOs) and lines of effort (LOEs), direct and indirect approach, anticipation, operational reach, culmination, arranging operations, and forces and functions.

b. **Termination.** Urban areas have their own underlying political, cultural, and religious forces that can affect conditions for **termination**. Termination requires an orderly transition to civilian control, either local or otherwise. During stability operations many considerations such as FHA, level and quality of government services, capability of indigenous forces, administration, and security will influence the nature and timing of transition to civilian control. The complexity of a JUO requires transition planning to be an integral part of operational planning and mission analysis. Transferring control of an operation is situationally dependent. In JUOs, partial or full transition may occur in one part of an urban area while operations continue in another. In crisis response and limited contingency operations, quick and efficient transition may be a critical mission objective, and thus a fundamental goal is setting the conditions for transition. In all operations, it is essential that routine activities such as providing sanitary services, food, law enforcement, utilities management, and health services be returned to civilian agencies as quickly as possible because of the demand they can place on joint force resources. An exit strategy is usually thought of in terms of military redeployment. However, until the local authorities have established a relatively safe and secure environment, law enforcement unit, a judicial presence, and a recognized and functioning governmental office with oversight of civilian reconstruction efforts, US capabilities (both military and nonmilitary) may continue to be required.

c. **Military End State.** In general, the end state of operations in urban environments is the termination of operations after strategic and operational objectives are achieved. This may include the transfer of routine responsibilities over the urban area from military to civilian authorities, another military force, or NGOs and IGOs.

d. **Objectives.** The JFC should continuously work to identify, understand, and articulate the military conditions necessary to achieve the strategic objectives. The tactical objectives must nest within and support the JFC's operational objectives but may be unique to the system resident in the specific urban environment. Objectives with regard to civilians should be considered including the desired physical and psychological condition of the civilian populace upon termination. Another military consideration is the follow-up political exploitation of completed military action and the military role in the transition to peace or stability operations. This exploitation includes matters such as CMO and FHA, and requires planning, liaison, and coordination both at the national level and in theater among diplomatic, military, political, NGO, and IGO leadership.

e. **Effects.** Joint operation planning uses the operational design element of **effects** to help clarify the relationship between objectives and tasks. The use of the operational design element of **effects** in conjunction with a systems perspective of the operational environment helps the JFC and staff determine the best combination and integration capabilities to accomplish tasks that create the right conditions to achieve objectives. For example, in most urban area operations the destruction of structures such as places of worship, medical facilities, and utilities will create long-term adverse results because of their importance to the general morale and welfare of the populace. (This consideration is in addition to the law of war issues with targeting religious sites and medical facilities.) This situation could hinder the joint force's ability to accomplish its mission. Unless the mission and objectives dictate otherwise, the JFC could establish a broad desired effect (condition), such as "Basic services for the populace remain operational." To support this effect, planners can establish ROE that restrict the use of destructive capabilities in specific areas. Planners also could develop tasks that require joint force components to protect specified facilities from enemy action.

f. **COG.** Crucial to the commander's ability to organize, arrange, and employ forces in JUOs is the accurate identification and analysis of the adversaries' COGs at each level of war. When considering the desired strategic end state, an urban area may be the strategic COG. Because major urban areas may house the centers of government, primary means of communications, and the hub of national culture, JFCs must determine whether an urban area itself is a COG or whether a strategic or operational COG (e.g., population) is located

CHECHNYA—IDENTIFYING THE CENTER OF GRAVITY

In assumptions based on a strategic intelligence assessment caused Russian commanders to incorrectly identify the rebel leadership as the Chechen strategic center of gravity—the primary source of their strength and power. In reality, ethnic nationalism, the true center of gravity, ran much deeper than the rebel leadership itself. Moreover, the Russians identified rebel leader Dudayev's personal security as a critical vulnerability at the operational level. They believed that by removing Dudayev (which they felt was a relatively easy task), they could readily put an end to the Chechen separatist movement. As an extension of this reasoning, they viewed Grozny, Dudayev's seat of government and the region's major transportation and industrial hub, as a decisive point. Thus, Grozny became the initial operational objective.

SOURCE: Timothy L. Thomas, The Battle of Grozny:
Deadly Classroom for Urban Combat, *Parameters,* Summer 1999

within that urban area or outside the urban area, but with a strong influence on it. Conversely, the COG may be resident in the urban area, but crosses into different areas and is to be targeted in a particular urban environment. In the latter case, planners should focus targeting to ensure the COG is recognized as a key objective. Once JFCs identify the COG, they must decide how the forces at their disposal can be applied in the most effective manner. The JFC should consider critical factors (capabilities, requirements and vulnerabilities) inherent in civil aspects of the operational environment, such as health, food, water, and sanitation. Since the JFC will base the operation plan largely on this identification, a thorough knowledge and understanding of all aspects of the urban area is of great importance. An operational COG within the urban area may be physical, psychological, or social. It may be adversary forces and capabilities, key infrastructure, the civilian population, individual, group, relationship, or other social factor/interaction or aspects of each. The JFC must use knowledge and understanding of both the adversary and the urban area to identify and then destroy, defeat, or neutralize the COG. The JFC must also anticipate and influence those events that may affect the friendly COG, such as public opinion.

g. **DPs. DPs** may be geographical, but are not necessarily traditional military terrain features, particularly in urban environments. They are not a COG; they are the keys to attacking the protected COG. They may be key cultural or political locations or locations of key infrastructure. They may also be psychological, such as the co-opting of a key tribal leader, avoiding activities which antagonize the population (entering religious buildings or sites, defaming historical sites, culturally inappropriate interaction with women) in order to undermine the influence of the main adversary leader or the molding of public opinion in friendly favor.

h. **LOOs and LOEs**

(1) As JFCs visualize the design of the operation, they may use several LOOs to help visualize and organize key operational elements/themes, which lead toward achieving operational and strategic objectives. LOOs define the orientation of the force in time and

LINES OF OPERATION AND LINES OF EFFORT IN IRAQ

Commanders in Operation IRAQI FREEDOM have used four (i.e., security, governance, economic development, communications) or six (i.e., security, transition, governance, economics, rule of law, communications) lines of effort to orient operations. Provincial reconstruction teams used: increase effectiveness of legitimate authorities, decrease effectiveness of illegitimate entities, increase legitimacy of legitimate authorities, and decrease legitimacy of illegitimate entities as lines of effort.

Various Sources

space or purpose in relation to an adversary or objective. Combining LOOs and LOEs allows commanders to include nonmilitary activities in their operational design.

(2) An LOE links multiple tasks and missions using the logic of purpose—cause and effect—to focus efforts toward establishing operational and strategic conditions. LOEs are essential to operational design when positional references to an enemy or adversary have little relevance, such as in counterinsurgency or stability operations. In operations involving many nonmilitary factors, LOEs may be the only way to link tasks, effects, conditions, and the desired end state.

i. **Direct and Indirect Approach.** In considering whether to opt for **direct or indirect approach** of a COG, the JFC needs to understand the nature of the COG and its relation to the urban area.

j. **Anticipation** is just as important as planning, but the information required to correctly anticipate events is more difficult to obtain. HUMINT and an understanding of the social and political fabric of the area **may** outweigh technical means of gathering information.

k. **Operational Reach.** When considering the distance, direction, and duration across which the joint force can successfully employ military capabilities, urban areas are often significant aspects of an operation. Operations in urban areas may be conducted initially for the seizure of lodgments (e.g., ports, airfields, and railheads) that facilitate future operations or the approach of the joint force; they may also be conducted to secure LOCs that extend the operational reach of the force. Controlling urban areas can have significant impact on operational reach and approach.

l. **Culmination.** The nature of JUOs requires careful consideration of **culmination.** The severe drain that JUOs can have on resources can cause either attacker or defender to exhaust capabilities earlier than anticipated, lose national will or popular support to continue. This may lead to an early culmination both on the operational and strategic levels. The complexity of the urban environment will require logistical resupply be planned, sequenced, and protected throughout operations; yet remain flexible to provide emergency sustainment to prevent a mission or force from culminating prior to achieving the objectives. The JFC should leverage all sources of power to prevent diplomatic or economic stalemate that could exacerbate issues with the local populace or create a refugee situation.

m. **Arranging Operations.** JFCs must determine the best **arrangement of operations** to conduct the assigned tasks and joint force mission. This arrangement will often be a combination of simultaneous and sequential operations to dominate and create the desired conditions to attain the end state. Commanders consider such factors as geography of the operational area; logistic buildup, distribution capacity, and consumption rates; adversary reinforcement capabilities; and public opinion. These factors are often intensified in JUOs and can significantly affect considerations for arrangement. Operational pauses may be required when a major operation may be reaching the end of its sustainability. In JUOs, the planning for branches and sequels should consider the potential effects not only of adversary action, but also of such events as political changes, public reaction to press reports, suffering among civilians, damage to infrastructure or culturally important structures, and breakdown of order. How well planners can anticipate and plan for branches and sequels may in large part determine how closely the JFC attains the desired end state. Planners should consider factors such as simultaneity, depth, timing, and tempo when arranging operations.

(1) **Simultaneity and Depth.** The increase in time required to conduct operations in urban environments, the presence of civilians, and the constriction of the urban operational environment affect **simultaneity and depth**. Simultaneity will mean not only the conduct of combat operations against an adversary, but also the simultaneous conduct of stability operations. Depth in JUOs can extend outside the actual urban area or be measured in a matter of city blocks. The nature of the urban environment often requires different types of operations to occur simultaneously or in rapid sequence, sometimes in close proximity. A situation can easily arise where members of the same friendly unit may at one moment be feeding and clothing dislocated civilians, at the next holding two warring tribes apart, and the next fighting a highly lethal battle—all within the same urban area. In a larger context, the joint force may have to conduct FHA and other operations at the same time and in the same area where combat operations are taking place. Such action may not wait for the stabilize and enable civil authority phases, but may be an integral part of the overall operation. Urban combat will bring with it requirements normally associated with noncombat crisis response and limited contingency operations. Further, crisis response and limited contingency operations may very well entail urban combat (e.g., in Somalia in the early 1990s, a humanitarian operation ended in urban combat).

(2) **Timing and tempo** are potentially the factors most affected by the urban environment. The nature of the terrain, difficulties in communication, and the presence of civilians slows down the actions of land forces. Operational limitations intended to protect civilians and infrastructure may inhibit and/or delay joint operations. Slowing down the pace of operations and buying time are often priorities of the urban defender. More time may lead to more casualties and a greater chance of an intervening event influencing strategic objectives. The JFC must recognize that the speed of operations in urban areas, particularly ground operations, will probably be slower than that of other operations, but the operational tempo may be very high. The JFC must still achieve a synchronization and integration of timing and tempo that leaves the opponent unable to act effectively. The tempo with which the commander can react to events, take action, and maneuver the force is key to success in JUOs. When operations in urban areas are part of a larger campaign, the high operational tempo of these operations may be conducted at very different tempos

and timings, from operations conducted outside the urban area, making overall synchronization and integration difficult.

n. **Forces and Functions.** Defeating enemy forces and disrupting enemy functions that may be deeply entwined in the area's infrastructure is a considerable challenge for the JFC who must do so without causing unacceptable civilian suffering. To this end, the ability to take precise action is critical, whether that entails fires using precision munitions, direct action (DA) against specific targets, creating nonlethal effects on selected infrastructure, or some other type of action.

o. **Other Considerations.** Isolation of the urban area is critical to achieving leverage; therefore, US forces frequently use technological superiority to achieve leverage. However, the advantages afforded by technological superiority may be different in urban environments compared to other operational environments. Advanced sensors and chemical, biological, radiological, and nuclear (CBRN) defense technologies that include medical prophylaxis and treatments, will enable the JFC to minimize casualties to the joint force operating in an urban environment; however, the joint force is not equipped with CBRN defense medical and nonmedical protection for massive civilian casualties in an urban environment. Therefore, the JFC factors into account potential civilian casualties from CBRN, psychological impact on the population, and how the enemy may use disinformation regarding its CBRN use against the joint force. In planning for an operation in an urban area where the adversary may have CBRN, the JFC should assess with allies, multinational partners, and the HN, the availability of CBRN defense medical and nonmedical protection for civilian populations in the event of significant CBRN attacks against civilian urban populations. In addition, the JFC should be prepared to counter an adversary's disinformation campaign. Activities such as PA, key leader engagement, and CMO can also provide a force with greater leverage in operations conducted in urban environments. Operations that lead to physical, informational, and moral isolation, and that counter an adversary's disinformation spread throughout the urban environment, have a major impact on the ultimate success of JUOs. At the operational level, isolate means cutting the adversary off from the functions necessary to be effective and denying access to capabilities that enable the exercise of coercion, influence, potential advantage, and freedom of action. Isolation has both an external aspect of cutting off outside support and information and an internal aspect of cutting off mutual support. Isolating the adversary also includes precluding any retreat.

(1) Isolation cannot be complete and indiscriminate, nor is it simply a matter of geographically surrounding an urban area with blocking positions or checkpoints (although it certainly may include that). Isolation attempts to close the openness of the urban environment with respect to support for the adversary—to choke off adversary growth from the outside so that joint operations are dealing with a fixed problem rather than one that continues to develop.

(2) Isolation involves identifying and controlling the most important ingress points into the urban area (and adapting as the adversary finds different routes). The level of granularity required in isolating an urban area will depend on the nature of the threat. In the case of a conventional adversary, it may require detecting and intercepting combat formations, while with an irregular adversary it may require intercepting individual

persons, civilian vehicles, or shipments. Isolation could involve the use of a wide variety of detection technologies and techniques (e.g., biometrics), especially those that can detect hostile persons, materiel, or information attempting to blend in with the general flow of the urban environment.

(3) **Physical isolation** involves interdicting the movement of units, persons, weapons, supplies, funds, contraband, and other shipments into the urban area. The physical isolation of a large urban area clearly has ground, air, space, and likely maritime implications for the identification and control of the movement of personnel and equipment. The capabilities provided by space-based C2, communications, and intelligence, surveillance, and reconnaissance (ISR) support systems may also be used to isolate urban areas. Physical isolation may not be limited to terrain. Isolation via denial of resources (e.g., power, water, food, ammunition, foreign support) may also be feasible, but requires close coordination with the servicing SJA to ensure compliance with the law of war.

(4) While physical isolation is very difficult, this is only one aspect of a larger issue. The JFC may also isolate the urban area in terms of information. Informational isolation involves interrupting hostile military, political, ideological, and financial or media communications. The JFC should have the capability to achieve and sustain **information superiority** over adversaries and potential adversaries. Information going into and out of the urban area should be under the control of the JFC as quickly and to the maximum extent possible. The joint force may not only cut off internal and external adversary communications, but may also control indigenous radio, television, and other media. One method to influence the information flow into and out of an urban area is to separate the adversary C2 system from its operational and strategic leadership. Informational isolation also can prevent the adversary from communicating with the civil population through television, radio, telephone, and computer systems. The overall result is to prevent adversary unity of effort within the urban area.

(5) **Moral isolation** is a function of both actions and the reaction by the larger community (e.g., other states, civilian populations) and can both deny the adversary political and military allies and separate the political leadership from the civilian populace. Moral isolation occurs when a force or individual violates rules of behavior they are expected to uphold (standards of conduct) and that violation is noticed and not forgiven by the larger community. The presence of legitimate international news organizations places special importance on the JFC's PA operations. The JFC's goals are thus to physically and psychologically isolate the adversary force and to ensure that the civilians in the area receive the JFC's messages and reject any messages from the adversary force. Similarly, joint force MISO may leverage the violations or moral isolation to influence adversary forces or decision makers.

5. Phasing

a. **General.** Arranging operations is an element of operational design, and phasing is a key aspect of this element. Phasing is a useful tool for any type of operation, from those that require large-scale combat to operations such as FHA, NEO, and peacekeeping. JUOs can normally be divided into phases to logically organize a campaign's or operation's diverse, extended, and dispersed activities. The primary benefit of phasing is that it assists commanders in systematically achieving objectives that cannot be achieved concurrently by arranging smaller, related operations in a logical sequence.

(1) Although the commander will determine the number and actual phases used during a JUO, the use of the six phases—shape, deter, seize initiative, dominate, stabilize, enable civil authority—provides a flexible model to arrange operations. Within the context of the phases established by a higher-level JFC, subordinate JFCs and component commanders may establish additional phases that fit their CONOPS. For example, the joint force land component commander (JFLCC) or a subordinate JTF might have the following four phases inside the combatant commander's (CCDR's) seize initiative phase: deploy, forcible entry, defense, and offense. The JFLCC could use the offense sub-phase as a transition to the CCDR's dominate phase.

(2) Operations in a single phase are unlikely to prove decisive in a JUO. Defeating a traditional military force in the dominance phase may not achieve strategic objectives and the desired end state until actions in the stabilization and enable civil authority phases are complete. Backward planning from enable civil authority is critical in this regard.

See JP 5-0, Joint Operation Planning, *for a more detailed discussion of the use of phasing in planning.*

b. **Considerations for Shaping, Deterrence, and Seizing the Initiative in Urban Areas.** Considerations for shaping, deterrence, and seizing the initiative in urban areas will only differ slightly from those of military operations conducted in other environments. The JIPOE products for specific urban areas will identify specific considerations that will apply.

c. **Considerations for Dominance in Urban Areas.** In combat operations, success requires full spectrum superiority of the operational environment through the seizure, disruption, control, or destruction of the adversary's critical factors, to include the operational and strategic COG. In JUOs, these may include tangible components of the infrastructure such as power grids, communications centers, transportation hubs, or basic services. They may also be intangible socioeconomic or political factors such as financial centers and capabilities, particular demographic groups and sites, and cultural sensitivities. Offensive operations may also mean controlling key terrain or infrastructure, disrupting the adversary's decision cycle, cutting or controlling intercity and intracity mobility and communications, triggering an adversary response, or positioning forces to conduct another phase. Defensive operations focus on denying the adversary control of those same DPs and the COG. The goal is not just movement to positions inside a city. The goal is to apply strength against the adversary's weakness, using tempo as a weapon to shatter adversary cohesion, organization, command, and psychological balance. Similarly, joint forces must learn to organize and integrate ground, maritime, air, and special operations combat power in the city, and to design and execute the sustainment schemes, including the use of precision aerial delivery, that build and maintain tempo. Both offensive and defensive operations in urban environments will probably entail heavy use of PA and CMO.

d. **Considerations for Stabilization in Urban Areas.** The focus of stabilization in an urban area is an ongoing process of organizing and strengthening the joint force position with respect to the urban area, combined with controlling the adversary within it. Stabilization also requires activities geared at neutralizing bypassed adversary forces and processing adversary prisoners.

(1) Stabilization may place heavy emphasis on logistic support and CMO. The nature of the urban environment ensures that the JFC will have to contend with issues concerning physical damage, civilians, and infrastructure as part of stabilization. Units conducting CMO may continue to be especially critical in this aspect, as well as engineering efforts ranging from destruction to repairs to new construction. Equally important are the expected issues of infrastructure collapse and the tasks of FHA and disaster relief. The rapid restoration of essential services to the population is critical to the stabilization effort. JFCs should ensure that sufficient resources are allocated to this effort.

(2) **CMO Planning Considerations**

(a) CMO planning must carefully consider the nature of the urban area and the specific operation to be conducted. For example, if the JFC considers administrative, logistic, and communications interoperability support requirements, additional requirements necessitated by the urban area must be considered by the JFC, both for CMO support and for support of other aspects of the operation. Where CMO is the primary focus of the operation, the JFC may wish to establish a joint CMO task force.

(b) CMO planners should carefully consider those aspects of the urban area— terrain, human, and infrastructure—that may impact CMO, in addition to potential human or environmental threats. Some of these planning factors include legal implications, communications, culture, education, economic, religious, labor, health, and administrative considerations. Since these factors are also key items of intelligence planning, CMO planning should be closely coordinated with intelligence efforts.

e. **Considerations for Enabling Civil Authority for Urban Areas.** Considerations for enabling civil authority for urban areas is the same as for other areas and will only differ based on specifics of the urban area involved.

6. **Other Operation Considerations for Urban Areas**

a. **Special Operations**

(1) **General**

(a) Special operations forces (SOF) give the JFC the flexibility to tailor a response to meet a wide range of potential urban requirements. Unique SOF capabilities can support the JFC's campaign and can achieve results not always attainable with the application of a larger conventional force. SOF also can enhance the JFC's unity of effort by providing trained, culturally aware, language proficient, military liaison personnel with communications that can offer the JFC a conduit to multinational forces operating under the

JFC or in concert with the operation. The day-to-day regional access SOF provides the JFC accurate information and area assessments to enhance situational awareness.

(b) Although the complexities of the urban environment change the way missions are conducted, SOF can perform core operations and activities in an urban environment unilaterally or in conjunction with conventional forces. These core operations and activities may be conducted across the range of military operations.

For further information, refer to US Special Operations Command Publication 3-33, Conventional Forces and Special Operations Forces Integration and Interoperability Handbook and Checklist, *and JP 3-05,* Special Operations.

(2) **Special Operations Capabilities in Urban Environments**

(a) **DA.** DA entails short-duration strikes and other small-scale offensive actions conducted as special operations in hostile, denied, or diplomatically sensitive environments, and which employ specialized military capabilities to seize, destroy, capture, exploit, recover, or damage designated targets. DA differs from conventional offensive actions in the level of diplomatic or political risk, the operational techniques employed, and the degree of discriminate and precise use of force to achieve specific objectives. In the urban environment, this precision strike capability is invaluable to limit collateral damage and civilian casualties.

(b) **Special Reconnaissance (SR).** SR entails reconnaissance and surveillance actions conducted by special operations in hostile, denied, or diplomatically sensitive environments to collect or verify information of strategic or operational significance, employing military capabilities not normally found in conventional forces. These actions

SPECIAL OPERATIONS FORCES IN PANAMA, 1989

Special operations forces (SOF) were involved in Panama throughout the entire campaign, and included Army Special Forces, Army Rangers, Army Special Operations Aviation, Naval Special Warfare, and Air Force Special Operations Forces. SOF participated in almost every action during Operation JUST CAUSE including infiltration, special reconnaissance, precision strike, and underwater demolition. These small, highly skilled units conducted attacks, often supported by AC-130 gunships, and were able to penetrate densely populated operational areas successfully as quick reaction forces. Before the airborne landing, SOF helped to prepare the battlefield and then reinforced the main effort once the airborne attack was over. Other uses of SOF included the attachment of psychological operations and civil affairs personnel to various task force units to serve as advisors, translators, liaisons, and assist in refugee control. This proved highly effective and aided in reestablishing law and order, promoting stability, and assisting in the establishment of a new Panamanian government. SOF capabilities can be force multipliers in the multifaceted urban environment.

SOURCE: *Joint Military Operations Historical Collection*

provide an additive collection capability for commanders and supplement other conventional reconnaissance and surveillance actions. SR may include collecting information on activities of an actual or potential enemy or securing data on the meteorological, hydrographic, or geographic characteristics of a particular area. SR may also include assessment of chemical, biological, residual nuclear, radiological, or environmental hazards in a denied area. SR includes target acquisition, area assessment, and post-strike reconnaissance, and may be accomplished by air, land, or maritime assets. In an urban environment, it is often difficult to gain accurate observation and surveillance through technological means. SOF, however, can provide visual observation to obtain or verify information and can emplace sensors in key locations. SOF SR can provide a form of HUMINT to supplement other sources of information. SR missions that may support operations in urban areas include environmental reconnaissance, armed reconnaissance, target and threat assessment, and post-strike reconnaissance.

b. **IO.** IO entail the integrated employment, during military operations, of information-related capabilities in concert with other LOOs to influence, disrupt, corrupt, or usurp the decision making of adversaries and potential adversaries while protecting our own. When properly coordinated, integrated, and synchronized as a part of JUO, IO affect the quality, content, and availability of information available to decision makers. IO also influence the perceptions and motivations of targeted key audiences with the goal of convincing them to act in a manner conducive to established objectives and desired end states.

c. **Foreign Consequence Management (FCM)**

(1) FCM in urban areas may include population evacuation, decontamination, transportation, communications, public works and engineering, firefighting, mass care, resource support, health and medical services, urban search and rescue (SAR), hazardous materials control, food distribution, and energy provision. Industries that work with TIMs near urban centers may need to be secured to avoid unintentional release or prevent a terrorist attack. As with almost all USG involvement within foreign nations, DOS serves as the lead agency in FCM operations with DOD in support.

(2) The complex physical urban terrain becomes even more complex in a CBRN environment. Buildings and public areas can be contaminated by chemical, biological, and radiological dispersal devices, and in the case of some biological agents carried throughout a building by way of the building's heating, ventilation, and air conditioning system, contaminated material, and person-to-person contact. The introduction of virulent and highly communicable diseases into an urban environment, with rail, road, ship, and air connections with the rest of the country, could be a major catastrophe. Subways and interior spaces offer ideal areas for limited chemical or biological attacks. Nuclear attacks can produce catastrophic results due to the effects of blast, thermal radiation, ionizing radiation, and residual radiation. The urban terrain can hinder rescue and relief efforts, either because of destruction or simply because of urban complexities, and significant engineering efforts may be required as part of CBRN response. Provision of logistics support also becomes extremely complex in urban environments. Both transportation of sustainment capabilities and supplies and the removal of waste and remains (particularly if contaminated) when the transportation system is degraded due to damage, contamination, or population density

requires unique planning and support of multiple agencies. Both DOS and DOD coordinate with NGOs and IGOs and, most important, the HN organizations, to better understand the capabilities and requirements of the HN.

(3) A CBRN incident can cause the population to panic requiring civilian authorities to restore order as well as provide relief services. Sizable numbers of dislocated civilians can clog the transportation system and overload support capabilities. The size and nature of the event, the capabilities of the HN, and the effects on the civilian population will have an influence on the type and amount of response a joint force will provide.

(4) Infrastructure also affects the CBRN response requirements. An event involving physical destruction may affect medical services, sanitation, power, communications, and law enforcement. Even if physical damage is limited, casualties and displacement of civilians may overload local and regional capabilities, particularly in less developed nations. The HN and local government capabilities may only be able to provide limited response in only certain areas and none in others.

(5) A number of special considerations are important in urban CBRN response. Figure III-2 depicts CBRN consequence management planning factors.

(a) Port and airfield facilities may be affected and therefore unusable or operate at a reduced capacity until repaired.

(b) Dispersion patterns are affected by the urban terrain and more difficult to predict and monitor.

(c) C2 is complicated by the nature of the urban area, being in a supporting role to DOS and HN civilian authorities, and the likely presence of NGOs.

(d) Requirements for decontamination, medical services, and basic life support may overwhelm the force's capabilities, even with augmentation of personnel and equipment from the continental US.

(e) Urban areas often include manufacturing plants, which may be a source of TIMs. These hazardous materials might be used to improvise CBRN weapons for use against the joint force or other people in the urban area.

Refer to JP 3-41, Chemical, Biological, Radiological, and Nuclear Consequence Management, *for detailed considerations when the JFC must conduct CBRN response operations.*

d. **FHA**

(1) **FHA consists of DOD activities, normally in support of the United States Agency for International Development (USAID) or DOS, to relieve or reduce human suffering, disease, hunger, or privation. FHA operations are limited in scope and duration.** Because of the numbers and density of civilians, a significant CMO (civil affairs

Chemical, Biological, Radiological, and Nuclear
Consequence Management Planning Factors

- Scope of the anticipated mission

- Anticipated threat during deployment, employment, and redeployment

- Estimated reaction time

- Physical characteristics of the urban area—size, natural topography, urban pattern and construction, and any special characteristics

- Demographics and characteristics and situation of the civilian population, to include considerations of law enforcement and population control

- Political situation in the urban area, region, and nation

- Available support from host nation, including infrastructure, equipment, and supplies

**Figure III-2. Chemical, Biological, Radiological, and Nuclear
Consequence Management Planning Factors**

operations [CAO]) effort on the part of the joint force may be required. However, the primary responsibility for US response to FHA requirements lies within the USAID.

(2) Most operations in urban areas will have a requirement for FHA. Some degree of assistance may be undertaken in concert with combat operations, peacekeeping, or other operations whose intent is not the provision of FHA. Because a United Nations or US civilian framework may not exist within which the JFC can support FHA, the joint force may need to perform immediate-response FHA.

(3) When assigned an FHA mission in an urban area, the JFC should take into consideration the characteristics of the urban area when planning the operation. When FHA is not assigned as part of an operation, the JFC should be prepared to conduct FHA if directed. These preparations should include the readiness to assess the nature and extent of humanitarian requirements in the urban area, to include available food and water, civilian casualties and loss of life, dislocated civilian population and location, status of local government or authority, and degree of destruction to property and infrastructure.

(4) **Urban FHA Considerations**

(a) Particularly during combat operations in urban environments, it may be difficult to provide relief for the civilian populace. There may be no agency immediately available to accept primary responsibility for FHA. By necessity, the JFC may find that the joint force must perform some FHA, and possibly provide extensive support, as well as conduct combat operations.

(b) The urban environment will affect the ability to conduct FHA. The same tendency toward fragmentation, hindrances to movement and communications, proximity of the press, and security requirements that accompany other types of operations conducted in urban areas will also affect urban FHA.

(c) Interagency coordination is key to successful FHA. Normally, the accessibility of urban areas makes it easier for NGOs and IGOs to participate, therefore increasing the number of agencies with which the joint force must deal.

(d) FHA requirements are more concentrated in urban areas, but so are the dangers: disease spreads more rapidly, unrest is more concentrated, rivalries are exacerbated by close contact, media attention is more pervasive, security is more problematic, and the population is significantly denser.

(5) **PRC**

(a) PRC normally assists HN governments or de facto authorities in retaining control over their population centers, thus precluding complicating problems that may hinder accomplishment of the JFC's mission. However, civil authorities may be either unable or unwilling to undertake responsibility for controlling the civilian population, in which case the joint force may have to conduct PRC alone or in coordination with civilian agencies. In friendly areas, these operations are conducted with the consent of the local government; in hostile territory, PRC is conducted in accordance with international law and the law of war.

(b) Successful PRC mobilizes and provides security for the population and material resources of an urban area. It can deny an adversary ready access to the population and to both internal and external sources of supply. PRC measures seek to reduce, relocate, or access populace and resources that may impede or otherwise threaten the success of military and supporting logistic operations.

(c) Populace control measures normally used in PRC include curfews, movement restrictions, travel permits, registration cards, and resettlement. Resource control measures can include licensing, regulations, checkpoints, ration controls, and inspection of facilities. In urban areas, however, the size and density of the civilian populace add a number of complications to PRC operations.

(d) **Urban PRC Considerations**

1. The potential magnitude of the PRC task in urban areas cannot be overstated. The JFC could be at least partially responsible for the care and control of hundreds of thousands, if not millions, of civilians, no matter what the original mission.

2. With the potential of huge numbers of civilians, urban PRC will be difficult to enforce. The standard control measures of passes, permits, and resettlement may be beyond the capabilities of the joint force for some time.

3. The JFC must give great care in the establishment of population control measures, depending on the situation and characteristics of that population. Inappropriate controls could exacerbate the PRC problem.

4. PRC measures must take into consideration the presence of factions, ethnic groups, and criminal organizations that may be hostile to one another or to the joint

POPULACE AND RESOURCES CONTROL OPERATIONS—BELFAST, 1921–PRESENT

While civilians are always a factor in urban operations, controlling the civilian population of Belfast is actually the primary focus of the entire operation and is integral to achieving stability. Because the conflict does not have distinguishable uniformed combatants, but rather draws its combatants from the civilian population, controlling and influencing the populace is key to identifying combatants, pre-empting and deterring violence, and stemming support for terrorist activities. More broadly, although stability can be temporarily created by force, long-term stability is ultimately dependent on changed popular perceptions, attitudes, and behavior. The task of controlling the civilian population while fighting terrorism has proved challenging for British forces not only because "combatants" are difficult to identify, but also because overly aggressive enforcement to root out combatants risks the danger of provoking the civilian populace toward militancy. Moreover, the nature of the mission has required British forces to perform a range of "police" functions that are atypical of normal military duties.

The key to controlling the urban population has been the synchronization of military and police responsibilities within the city. The nature of stability operations has blurred the line normally present between military and police objectives. While the Royal Ulster Constabulary (RUC) is the law enforcement agency within Northern Ireland, it has evolved into more of a paramilitary force in order to deal with the extreme cases of violence in the city. To support the RUC properly, British commanders have adapted their military force to accomplish both military and police tasks. For example, British forces have modified their intelligence units to enable tracking of informants, often exploiting typical police tools such as working dogs. Special Air Service units have adopted many of the functions of a special weapons and tactics team to extract terrorists. More generally, British forces have taken on basic policing duties such as street patrolling.

To accomplish their tasks, the military forces in Northern Ireland have been granted special legal and police powers, to include the authority to:

- Stop and question any person about his identity and movements

- Stop and search any person for weapons

- Arrest without warrant and detain for four hours

- **Enter premises and search with only the permission of a commissioned officer**

- **Stop vehicles/vessels for search**

- **Control and restrict highways, rights of way, and access to buildings**

Exercise of these powers has been instrumental in enabling the British forces to assist the RUC in maintaining a stable environment. However, in some instances, real or perceived abuses of these powers have incited the local populace. The nationalists (and some loyalists) have always felt these "special powers" were too broad and allowed the soldiers to violate their civil rights. In recognition of these sentiments, British commanders have generally been extremely careful in monitoring the use of these powers and ensuring that their soldiers do not abuse them. The British rules of engagement (ROE) have allowed their soldiers to use reasonable force to prevent a crime or assist in the lawful arrest of offenders or suspected offenders. Violations of ROE by British soldiers have been prosecuted under United Kingdom law, and the offenders have been punished, although too lightly in the eyes of some factions. Despite some criticism, the British have been generally successful in exercising control of the urban population without provoking popular backlash by their presence. In large part, they have done this by adapting to the exigencies of the mission and by coordinating extensively with their police counterparts.

The British performance in Belfast provides a model of both inter-Service and inter-agency cooperation. Militarily, the British have established a solid chain of command based on regional areas in which all members of the armed forces are subordinate. The integration of regular Army forces with special forces, intelligence, and explosive ordnance disposal units has been seamless. The British have also done a remarkable job interfacing with the local RUC units, and have effectively modified their forces to perform police functions.

SOURCE: *Handbook for Joint Urban Operations*

force. Further, these groups may have ways of controlling their members that are not readily apparent to the joint force.

     <u>5.</u> The complexities of the physical urban terrain could result in fragmentation of effort and difficulty in imposing controls in a consistent manner throughout the urban area. Physical aspects of urban terrain can hamper CMO.

     <u>6.</u> Security of civilians could be difficult and require significant resources.

     <u>7.</u> There is a strong potential for the use of civilians by the adversary. This use can range from using them as human shields to fomenting riots to conducting terrorist attacks on civilians to influence US policy and actions.

        8. As with any dealings with the civilian population, PRC operations require an understanding of the culture.

        9. The objectives of PRC are to move civilians away from combat areas or other areas of concern within the city, to centralize them into one or more locations, to provide for their basic needs, and to foster cooperation and good will.

        (e) **Operations involving dislocated civilians can be a special category of PRC.** In situations of crisis and adversity, whether from war or other cause, people converge on urban areas from the surrounding regions, so it is possible that the commencement of operations in urban areas will find dislocated civilians already present. Urban combat will create many more displaced persons, either through design or as an inadvertent result of urban fighting.

For further guidance on FHA, refer to JP 3-29, Foreign Humanitarian Assistance.

        e. **Urban SAR Program.** The US Army Corps of Engineers Urban SAR program provides technical and operational support to the Federal Emergency Management Agency urban SAR program and other state, local, and international urban SAR programs. The US Army Corps of Engineers leads the training for structures specialists, and maintains a cadre of structures specialists deployed as part of incident support team engineering cell, and urban SAR task forces.

        (1) Urban SAR is a dangerous undertaking when conducted in buildings that are fully or partially collapsed. Typically, these structures are multistoried and contain heavy debris with a high potential for additional collapse. Engineers trained as structures specialists can evaluate a damaged building in order to reduce the risks to rescue personnel and victims. Structures specialists design shoring systems to stabilize structures for rescuers to gain safe access to the victims. The structures specialists are trained in Rescue Systems 1 (a basic rescue skills course), critical incident stress awareness and management, and hazardous material awareness. They also receive instruction in structural collapse patterns, hazard identification and building monitoring, rapid assessment of buildings, building triage and marking systems, and advance shoring and shoring calculations.

        (2) The US Army Corps of Engineers structures specialist cadre is an essential component of the urban SAR task forces and the incident support team with the ability for fast deployment in a life-saving mission. The structures specialist brings engineering expertise to the urban SAR task force. Responsible for evaluating the immediate structural conditions at the incident and recommending the appropriate hazard mitigation, the structures specialist serves a vital function to the task force.

Intentionally Blank

CHAPTER IV
JOINT FUNCTIONS

"In Somalia, Lebanon, and Iraq, the enemy also learned that America's vulnerable center of gravity is dead American soldiers. Thus, killing Americans has gravitated from merely a means to an end to an end itself, and the most efficient killing ground is in cities, where urban clutter allows the enemy to hide. Familiar terrain, the presence of supporting populations, and a useful infrastructure gives the enemy the advantage of sanctuary in the midst of the occupying power, an advantage impossible to achieve in open terrain. He can literally hide in plain sight and become indistinguishable from the indigenous urban masses that shield, protect, and sustain him."

Urban Warfare: A Soldier's View
Major General Robert H. Scales, US Army, Retired, 2005

1. General

a. Joint functions are related capabilities and activities grouped together to help JFCs integrate, synchronize, and direct joint operations. Functions that are common to joint operations at all levels of war fall into six basic groups—C2, intelligence, fires, movement and maneuver, protection, and sustainment. A number of subordinate tasks, missions, and related capabilities help define each function. Some tasks, missions, and capabilities could apply to more than one joint function.

b. In any joint operation, the JFC can choose from a wide variety of joint and Service capabilities and combine them in various ways to perform joint functions and accomplish the mission. This chapter discusses the key considerations related to the application of joint functions and their related tasks in an urban environment.

2. Command and Control

a. **General**

(1) The ability of the JFC to influence the outcome of operations conducted in urban areas is the result of leadership and the ability to control forces and functions in order to execute the intent. C2 is supported by reliable and secure communications systems. These systems process and integrate data and information, pass it to where it is needed, and display it in a usable format in time to be acted upon. This combination of C2 and the tools for its implementation is fundamental to the conduct of modern military operations. The nature of the urban environment accentuates the challenges to the JFC, and offers significant hindrances to effective C2.

(2) It is more challenging to understand and shape the operational environment in an urban area than in other environments. The key to understanding the urban operational environment at all levels is the ability to rapidly collect and disseminate information. Urban areas contain a great deal of uncertainty, and since knowledge is a perishable asset, then

speed and precision are necessary to get the right information in the right hands as expediently as possible.

b. **C2 Considerations in JUOs**

(1) The complex physical urban terrain inhibits the performance of some technologies supporting C2, including LOS communications and overhead surveillance. Subterranean and interior spaces make timely knowledge and understanding of the urban operational environment more difficult. Figure IV-1 illustrates these challenges.

(2) The presence of civilians further complicates C2. The JFC must consider the effects of operations on civilians, and their presence in large numbers will require greater attention to areas such as interagency support, CMO, and PA.

(3) Existing infrastructure such as transportation and communication systems can both facilitate and hinder C2. Service infrastructure such as police, fire, and medical services may offer control and intelligence opportunities, but its absence will certainly add to the requirements of the joint force.

(4) **As ground operations tend to become decentralized,** it is important that C2 be flexible, adaptive, and decentralized as well. Essential to decentralized C2 is the thorough knowledge and understanding of the **commander's intent** at every level of command. To further enhance decentralized C2, commanders at all levels should issue **mission-type orders** and use **implicit communications** wherever possible.

(5) The **commander's critical information requirements** categories of friendly, adversary, and environmental information must also include pertinent information concerning the urban environment. Friendly information may include items such as anticipated political actions by an HN, the ability of the HN to support civilians, or the presence of sufficient precision munitions in the joint force. Although the adversary may

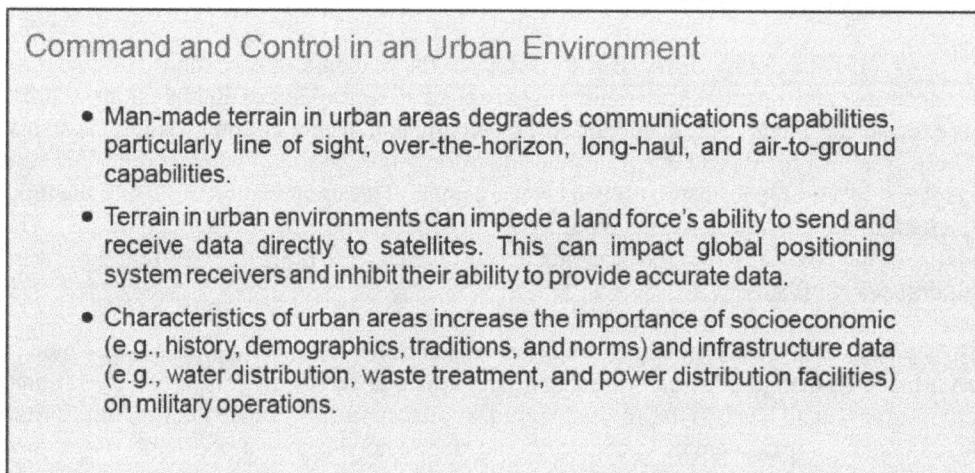

Command and Control in an Urban Environment

- Man-made terrain in urban areas degrades communications capabilities, particularly line of sight, over-the-horizon, long-haul, and air-to-ground capabilities.

- Terrain in urban environments can impede a land force's ability to send and receive data directly to satellites. This can impact global positioning system receivers and inhibit their ability to provide accurate data.

- Characteristics of urban areas increase the importance of socioeconomic (e.g., history, demographics, traditions, and norms) and infrastructure data (e.g., water distribution, waste treatment, and power distribution facilities) on military operations.

Figure IV-1. Command and Control in an Urban Environment

GROZNY—PROBLEMS IN COMMAND AND CONTROL

Command and control is especially important in a joint urban operation when coordination of forces is required to negotiate a complex environment. Russian command and control was convoluted, resulting in poor synchronization of Russian forces during the 1994-95 battle for Grozny. Russian units had no unity of command; command was scattered between the Ministry of the Interior, the Ministry of Defense, and the Federal Counterintelligence Service, the successor to the KGB. Commanders did not coordinate with Russian units on their flanks. In fact, they moved in almost autonomous columns along four main routes. The organization and sequencing of force caused many command and control problems for Russian troops. For example, General Anatoly Kvashin commanded the Main Assault Force that entered Grozny from the north. As Kvashin advanced, Chechen rebels focused most of their firepower on his force because, unknown to Kvashin, the Russian commanders from the east and west gave false reports about their whereabouts. It was not until the second day of the operation that Kvashin realized that he was fighting in the city without the help of Groups East and West.

On the other side, Chechen mobility and innate knowledge of the city exponentially increased their ability to command and control their forces. The Chechens generally did not maintain strongholds, but remained mobile. Hit and run tactics made it very difficult for the Russian force to locate pockets of resistance and impossible to bring its overwhelming firepower to bear against the enemy force. Moreover, high-rise buildings and structures impeded Russian transmissions, especially those in the high frequency and very high and ultra high frequency ranges, making it difficult to communicate unit locations. The Chechens overcame this problem by using cellular phones and commercial scanner systems, which allowed them to communicate easily with one another and ensured the coordination of their combat operations.

SOURCE: Timothy L. Thomas, The Battle of Grozny: Deadly Classroom for Urban Combat, *Parameters*, Summer 1999

consist of a traditional armed force, priority intelligence requirements on criminal elements, guerrillas, terrorists, and tribal or political factions may be necessary. Environmental information requirements may include elements of the urban environment, such as the behavior and needs of civilians or the presence or likelihood of disease or hunger.

(6) In JUOs, it is likely that a **JOA** will be established that will include the urban area and sufficient surrounding area for the joint force to achieve its objectives. The AOI should include any area from which influence can be exerted on the urban area. Other operational areas may be designated outside or inside the JOA. Maneuver and movement control measures must be carefully considered and delineated to allow maximum flexibility on the part of subordinate commanders and to prevent friendly fire.

(7) The **joint force headquarters should be organized** based on the nature and requirements of the operation. The JFC may need to establish cross-functional organizations specifically tasked to deal with some aspect of the operation. In particular, the JFC coordinates with multinational partners and other USG departments and agencies to facilitate cooperation, mutual support, and understanding. In urban areas, coordination will include HN agencies, local leadership (both official and unofficial), IGOs, and NGOs. The support of these organizations may be critical to the accomplishment of strategic and operational objectives. These groups can offer the JFC a wealth of information, knowledge, and insight concerning the particular urban area, and their cooperation may enhance the JFC's understanding of the area and provide critical assistance in dealing with local groups and the civilian populace. In any case, close support and cooperation will foster unified action and the attainment of the desired end state. The extensive liaison required during operations in urban areas means it is very likely many of these organizations will be represented in the force headquarters or liaison with the CMOC. The force may also provide liaison to them, as well as to HN agencies such as police or local government, different tribes, clans, or factions, or any other of the myriad groups that may be influential in a particular urban area.

(8) Depending on the type of operation, there will almost certainly be **operational limitations** placed on the JFC in the accomplishment of the strategic and operational objectives. In the development of ROE, the President and SecDef will provide guidance based upon input from the JFC and attempt to balance constraints, restraints, mission accomplishment, applicable law, and protection of the force. Based on experience from recent operations, future adversaries may try to take advantage of the fact that US military forces will comply with the law of war. In developing ROE, the commander must consider the potential for civilian casualties, collateral damage, or friendly casualties to influence the accomplishment of operational objectives.

See subparagraph 7.f., "Legal," for a discussion of the legal aspects of operations in urban areas.

c. **Communications.** The nature of the urban environment presents certain challenges to C2 and communications. Communications challenges are influenced by decentralization, the three-dimensional nature of the urban environment, urban hindrances to radio communications, and the existence of an urban communications infrastructure.

(1) The decentralization inherent in urban operations requires the ability to communicate quickly outside the normal communications patterns. Due to the complexity of urban terrain; maintaining situational awareness and developing a common operational picture are very difficult. The communications system must support the joint force throughout the entire urban terrain including the exterior and interior, surface and subsurface portions.

(2) **Radio communications** reliability is degraded in the urban environment by the presence of tall buildings, poorly maintained power distribution systems, a noisy electromagnetic environment, saturation of the radio frequency environment, and physical urban features that result in LOS obstructions, reducing radio link ranges. When developing the information management plan, considerations must be given to employing more ground-

based transceivers; augmenting ground-based systems with airborne relays; or using diverse radio modulation techniques to allow frequency spectrum reuse. The need to increase communications transceiver density in urban areas adds significantly to the equipment, resupply, and manpower requirements of engaged forces. At the very least, the JFC will need to provide a large amount of additional equipment to subordinate forces. **Existing communications systems** in an urban area may range from the very sophisticated to the rudimentary. However, all offer the possibility of use by the joint force to augment its organic communications capability, compensate for shortages, or meet early communications requirements during initial deployment. The JFC may be able to make efficient use of existing communications infrastructure, from basic telephone lines to video and data transmission. The urban environment presents an increased probability of capture of sensitive information. Information protection measures should also be considered as part of this infrastructure.

See JP 6-0, Joint Communications System, *for a full discussion of communications considerations.*

(3) As the single control agency for the management and operational direction of the joint communications network, the joint network operations control center **(JNCC) must know the requirements of communications in the urban environment, especially in the specific operational area**. The JNCC must be aware of the capabilities present, their potential use, and any problems associated with use. Vital to communications management is the need to support planning and execution to include information exchange requirements, radio frequency spectrum management and allocation, communications equipment dispersion, and continual assessment of communications effectiveness.

d. **Space Capabilities for C2**

(1) The same urban characteristics that interfere with the ability to communicate on the ground can diminish the information derived from space-based systems.

(2) Space systems may be employed to monitor an urban area before friendly forces are established.

(3) Space systems provide **C2 and communications.** Considering the difficulties in communications in and around urban areas, the C2 capability offers the JFC the ability to exchange information inside the urban area, between elements of the joint force, and also facilitates intertheater and intratheater communications. Space systems may form a critical link in the C2 architecture that rapidly passes data and information.

(4) The space-based **Global Positioning System (GPS)** provides position, navigation, and timing information that allows precise site surveys, emplacement of artillery, target acquisition, and location. However, the complex terrain and increased density of urban structures, such as multistory buildings (as well as jammers), can inhibit connectivity with and accuracy of GPS systems.

(5) The ability of space systems to provide terrain information and imagery is crucial to the success of land forces.

See JP 3-14, Space Operations, *for a full discussion of space operations.*

e. **Safety and Mishap Risk Management.** High-tempo operations may increase the risk of injury and death due to mishaps. Asphalt, concrete, and heights cause injuries not normally seen in large numbers in other types of terrain. JUOs in general also tend to produce a significant number of injuries due to the nature of the terrain—falls from walls or windows, vehicular injuries, injuries caused by contact with building walls. Cities pose their own safety hazards even in the absence of an enemy. Command interest, discipline, risk mitigation measures, and training lessen those risks. The JFC reduces the chance of mishap by conducting risk assessments, assigning a safety officer and staff, implementing a safety program, and seeking advice from local personnel. Safety considerations could include weather, local road conditions and driving habits, uncharted or uncleared mine fields, and special equipment hazards.

f. **PA**

(1) The density of media representatives in urban areas increases the likelihood of formal news media coverage of operations. Those hostile to US intentions may have unfettered access to mass media outlets to spread misinformation about operations and, as previously noted, much of the population may have the capability to capture and post images and information to the Internet or send them to the media in near real time. These possibilities demand an aggressive public communication effort by the joint force to put operational actions into context (before others have the chance to exploit them) or to counter erroneous information. PA participation throughout the planning, execution, and assessment process is critical to ensure that the public implication of operation plans are considered, addressed, and assessed.

(2) The proximity of cultural and political centers and the willingness of adversaries to exploit US actions makes it relatively easy for media representatives to find authoritative sources of information for stories about US operations without US support. The JFC must therefore plan and execute PA operations that media find credible and timely and serve as a valuable source of current news and information to reduce the need for the media to go elsewhere. Integration of PA is critical to the success of all military operations or campaigns, but even more important in an urban environment due to the proximity and abundance of observers and media.

g. **CMO**

(1) **General**

(a) CMO performed in urban areas will require a significant effort on the part of the joint force.

(b) Strategic CMO focus on long-term global and regional issues such as reconstruction, economic development, and stability. At the operational level, CMO support strategic CMO objectives and focus on near-term and immediate issues such as health service infrastructure, NEO, movement, feeding, and sheltering of dislocated civilians, police and security programs, building foreign nation government legitimacy, integration of interagency operations with military operations, and synchronization and integration of CMO support to tactical commanders.

(c) CMO in urban areas have three primary objectives.

1. Enhance military operations by minimizing civilian interference.

2. Support friendly or multinational forces objectives by assisting the HN in achieving its political, economic, and psychological objectives.

3. Integrate civil and military actions to help hasten an end to hostilities and attempt to limit collateral damage on indigenous populations and institutions (IPI) from offensive, defensive, or stability operations. These negative impacts can range from civilian casualties and loss of property to destruction of supporting infrastructure. The effects of civilian suffering often have a profound influence on the attainment of strategic and operational objectives. Commanders must meet the legal obligations and moral responsibilities to the civilian populations within the operational environment.

(2) **CMO Considerations in Urban Environments**

(a) It may be difficult to find and reach all those in need of support. Restricted terrain makes it more difficult to control large numbers of people in PRC operations. Although urban areas normally offer many buildings usable for shelter, medical care, and other forms of support, the damage to those structures from military operations or natural or man-made disasters can make them unusable, thus adding to the infrastructure support difficulties.

(b) Many civilians will be displaced and in need of basic support. Services may be degraded or nonexistent. The requirement to control and support the civilian population can easily overwhelm local capabilities. For example, at the onset of an operation in an urban area there might be a portion of the population without daily employment or activity, having literally nothing to do. This stagnant population is looking for some form of employment activity and can easily be influenced by the adversary to hinder or harm the operation. This very segment of the population can be used by the JFC as the resource to jumpstart the rebuilding of the urban environment. Temporarily employing this population not only denies the adversary a resource pool, but also starts the urban environment on the road to recovery. Urban areas are rarely homogeneous, and effective CMO will require understanding of the local culture, ethnicity, neighborhoods, tribal relations, and the basic allegiances and daily life of the inhabitants.

(c) Urban infrastructure may be functioning with some degree of effectiveness, in which case CA must work through and with local authorities and services. It may be necessary to repair physical infrastructure facilities and means, such as power plants or water stations, as part of CMO. Existing service infrastructure may be totally lacking or overwhelmed by circumstances, requiring the joint force to provide not only basic subsistence and shelter, but the full gamut of support personnel—security, legal, administration, engineer, sanitation, medical, transportation, and other.

(d) CMO can support overall operational objectives or be the focus of operations. CMO may be conducted to shape the operational environment, engage a civil problem, or assist in the transition to civil authority.

(e) JUOs will always require the conduct of CMO in one part of an urban area while another is still being contested in conventional combat, thus calling for close synchronization and integration of combat and CMO requirements and actions. CMO may take place in the urban area itself or, in the case of massive civilian displacement, in areas nearby.

(f) CMO will require support in a number of key areas from forces and organizations who themselves understand the nature of operations in urban environments.

1. **CA** staff, and supporting units, should form the nucleus of CMO planning efforts. CA forces are a multiplier for JFCs and can provide valuable information and analysis with respect to the civil component of the operational environment, as well as plan and execute targeted nonlethal operations focused at specific populations or civilian audiences within the urban area. CAO require a strong relationship between military forces, NGOs, IGOs, and IPI in the urban areas where military forces are present. CA forces can use the application of functional specialty skills that normally are the responsibility of civil government to enhance the conduct of CMO during urban operations.

2. **Engineering** support could be critical to CMO, particularly in combat and FHA operations. This support may consist of firefighting services, facilities repair and management, power generation, construction of fuels and water supply, erection of temporary shelter, construction and repair of ports and airfields, repair and maintenance of transportation and communications systems, explosive ordnance disposal, bridging, contingency construction/services contracting, and mapping/geospatial information and services, or many other actions.

3. **Health services** may be the most immediately critical asset of CMO. Health services in urban areas may consist of medical and dental treatment, preventive medicine services, medical logistics, training, and medical evacuation. In JUOs, health services activities should pay particular attention to the development of medical intelligence and threat analysis due to the strong potential for epidemic outbreaks.

4. **Transportation** support is necessary for the distribution of food, water, and medicines, for medical evacuation, and for the movement of dislocated civilians to a safe environment.

5. **Military police and security forces** may be vital to establishing sufficient control for CMO to successfully take place, as well as providing a normal law enforcement capability when none is present.

(g) CMO will occur simultaneously with other operations including combat, both defensive and offensive. CMO must be synchronized with all entities operating within the urban area to build synergy, unity of command, and the effective use of finite resources available to the commander.

HAITI—CIVIL-MILITARY OPERATIONS

The large civilian population in Port-au-Prince and the complexities of the humanitarian mission required the United States to interact constantly with other US governmental entities. These agencies included US Agency for International Development and the State and Justice Departments, along with a variety of nongovernmental organizations (NGOs) that also supported nation-building in Haiti. To help resolve the cultural and operational differences between the military and civilian organizations, the joint task force created a formal political-military operations plan that included a civil-military operations center (CMOC). US forces also established a humanitarian assistance coordination center as a part of the CMOC to serve as a clearinghouse for all humanitarian requests for assistance and to prevent NGOs from inundating the headquarters. Civil affairs and Army Special Forces personnel were instrumental in manning and facilitating these activities. In retrospect, the relative smoothness of the operation owes much to the intensity of civil-military cooperation that the CMOC helped to foster.

In addition to the CMOC, Military Information Support Teams (MISTs) were established in June of 1994 to support US policy to restore Haiti's democratic government, counteract misinformation broadcasts by Haiti's de facto military regime, and disseminate messages from Aristide to the Haitians. The MISTs were typically five-person teams composed of a military information support operations (MISO) [formerly psychological operations (PSYOP)] officer; a noncommissioned officer; two MISO [PSYOP] specialists with photography, videography, journalism, or editing skills; and a civilian analyst with linguistic and area specialist skills. The MISTs interacted with both US and host nation militaries and law enforcement agencies to develop appropriate MISO [PSYOP] missions, information campaigns, and military intelligence support.

SOURCE: *Joint Military Operations Historical Collection*

1. During defensive operations in urban areas, CMO contribute to the military effort by maintaining liaison with civil and interagency organizations and officials, which provides better situational awareness and contributes to force protection. Additionally, coordination with the international relief community can result in a diminution of requirements for US military support to nonmilitary missions, helping to conserve military resources. Finally, PRC measures minimize adversary access to the area (which supports force protection) as well as adversary access to HN logistic support. The commander must also consider the effects of defensive operations on the civilian populace and take the appropriate CMO measures.

2. CMO contributes to the military effort during offensive operations as well. Liaison with local officials and the local populace again provides an additional source of situational awareness, some of which can be used for the targeting of adversary forces and positions. Coordination with the relief community helps conserve military resources. Most importantly, PRC measures can be used to minimize civilian interference with military

operations, supporting the JFC's mobility requirements. Again, the JFC must consider the effects of operations on the civilian populace and conduct CMO both to support that populace and to enhance operational capabilities.

For additional information on CMO and CAO, refer to JP 3-57, Civil-Military Operations.

3. Intelligence

a. Intelligence activities in urban environments are significantly different from other environments because of the vast number of variables found in urban areas in comparison with the conventional operational environment. Numerous factors make JIPOE for urban areas a complex and detailed undertaking, including the nature of the urban environment. Attaining situational awareness, visualizing operations, and providing timely intelligence and information to support decision making are critical JIPOE functions in an urban environment. A detailed discussion of JIPOE for JUOs is found in Appendix A, "Joint Intelligence Preparation of the Operational Environment in Urban Areas." The density of the urban operational environment often requires vast amounts of intelligence received from many different sources and channels to be processed efficiently. Furthermore, to be effective in an urban environment, intelligence must be processed and disseminated to operating forces in real time. This method has been proven to enable operating forces to take advantage of opportunities garnered by the cascading effect of tactical successes, wherein information discovered during an ongoing operation in turn provides actionable intelligence for immediate follow-on actions. To properly fuse the breadth and depth of information and intelligence, additional resources may be required.

b. Intelligence on more than threat issues alone is important in JUOs. The desire to employ precision munitions and reduce collateral damage places increased demand on ISR systems to provide high-fidelity, geospatially accurate intelligence for targeting, in near-real time. Many adversaries will be non-uniformed irregular forces, employing nonmilitary vehicles, therefore reliance on HUMINT reporting and intelligence sensors that both detect and discriminate enemy from civilians will place increased demands on intelligence staffs at all levels.

c. Unmanned aircraft systems (UASs) play a major role in JUOs and provide a distinct advantage over other airborne collection assets. Their longer loiter times, persistent surveillance, ability to downlink directly to maneuver elements, and point targeting capabilities enable increased situational awareness to the commander.

d. **Information superiority** is an integral and necessary requirement for JUOs, and intelligence is one of the primary means to achieve it. During JUOs, the JFC relies on comprehensive intelligence to determine the social, political, and cultural environment, the physical terrain, adversary capabilities, demographics, and other characteristics of the urban operational environment.

e. Information requirements normally focus on adversary forces and the physical environment, but for operations in urban areas they must include detailed information concerning the nature and characteristics of the urban area—terrain, populace, and infrastructure as well as political, cultural, economic, and other considerations. These requirements will also have different priorities in JUOs, with intelligence concerning civilian population or infrastructure potentially as important as that concerning the adversary. Intelligence centers should work with the JFC to determine intelligence requirements, collecting information concerning the urban area(s) in the theater and JOA, and producing intelligence products that focus on a specific urban area for a specific operation. Among the areas for the centers' attention might be the threat, biographic information on urban civilian leaders, and economic, geographic, sociocultural, and political factors. Civil information management can contribute to this effort.

f. A large amount of the information needed to support JUOs is available well before a decision is made to commit US forces to a particular urban area. Information is often readily available on urban terrain, demographics, and infrastructure, but the precise and detailed information required to conduct operations may be more difficult to obtain. Geospatial intelligence (GEOINT) and signals intelligence (SIGINT) have often provided timely and fairly complete information to the commander, but both of these sources contain drawbacks when used to gather information in urban areas. GEOINT can provide a picture of the layout of a city, the functions of some structures, the location of communications sites, vehicular movement patterns, and other facilities and activities that can be viewed from the outside. Measurement and signature intelligence could provide information concerning the presence of certain elements such as WMD or other covert indications. The same is true of SIGINT. Experience in JUOs clearly indicates that HUMINT is essential in understanding the local behavior and psychology, pinpointing locations within structures or underground, identifying targets that cannot be seen by GEOINT, and developing situational awareness. While the reliability of information gained from HUMINT sources can be questionable, the information should be verified by other human sources or technical means. Counterintelligence (CI) is essential to prevent insider threats to and enhance the force protection of US forces in urban environments. CI also supports urban operations through the detection, identification, exploitation, and neutralization of the multidiscipline intelligence activities of competitors, opponents, adversaries, and enemies.

g. SOF and other joint reconnaissance assets can provide support to the JFC in the collection of operational information, including sociocultural and target intelligence. These assets may already be deployed to the JOA or can be deployed early to help bridge the gap between other forms of information and the current situation. The presence of these assets in the urban area can be beneficial in understanding and shaping the operational environment, target identification, and meeting critical information requirements.

h. Because urban terrain is primarily man-made, it is subject to frequent and substantial change, and maps and other representations can easily become out of date. In addition, maps and even near-real-time imagery are primarily two-dimensional, making **accurate visualization of the operational environment** difficult. Additionally, the urban terrain hampers geo-positioning by making it difficult to determine at any given time the exact locations of friendly forces. Accurate maps of the urban areas, in a scale useful at the lowest levels, and visual representations are a necessity in JUOs. Defense Intelligence Agency and National Geospatial-Intelligence Agency (NGA) gridded reference graphics are required to assist the air-to-ground coordination required for all combat air support missions such as CAS, resupply, air assault, infiltration, and exfiltration. These representations could take the form of line maps, images, image maps, three-dimensional perspective views, computer simulated fly-throughs, or other specialized representations of the operational environment. NGA currently provides numerous intelligence services and products to the joint force, including city maps with street names in both English and the native language, image city maps, traditional aerial imagery, and other products.

(1) The US Army Geospatial Center developed an expeditious process to analyze, map, and display layers of urban area information—in the Urban Tactical Planner.

MOGADISHU—INTELLIGENCE GATHERING

Every urban area is defined by a unique set of physical, social, economic, cultural, and historical circumstances. In Mogadishu, Somali social, economic, and political relations are mediated by an unwritten social code dictated by kinship and religious precepts. Even though Somalis share a single ethnic background, a single language, and a single religion (Sunni Islam), clan rivalry and a patrilineal hierarchy divide the country. These cultural differences contribute to a volatile political atmosphere in which clan personalities and historical relationships govern decision making. Understanding this foreign system of government significantly helped the joint force commander (JFC) of Operation RESTORE HOPE to make use of local assets and provided him with the situational awareness necessary to achieve mission success. In comparison, during United Nations (UN) Operation in Somalia (UNOSOM) II, US leaders failed to take certain factors of Somali culture into consideration, contributing to the operation's failure.

During Operation RESTORE HOPE, human intelligence (HUMINT) gathering was conducted on the ground in Mogadishu prior to the formation of unified task force (UNITAF). HUMINT sources developed relationships with official contacts, observed first-hand the dynamics of Somali politics, and were able to provide significant intelligence on militia activities. This type of HUMINT is essential in urban operations. Continuous monitoring of the local population's disposition and the adversary's intentions ensures that diplomatic and/or military efforts are appropriate to the situation and well received by relevant political leaders.

To track and disperse this type of intelligence, US forces established a civil-military operations center (CMOC) to serve as a clearinghouse for information between the humanitarian agencies and the multinational coalition force. The CMOC communicated daily with State Department Presidential Envoy Robert Oakley, a former US Ambassador to Somalia who knew most of the major Somali political players. Clearing a political path for the US-led relief effort, Oakley and a small staff traveled into southern Somalia explaining to local leaders what to expect as troops arrived at distribution sites.

The importance of understanding local politics and integrating indigenous decision makers into an urban operation cannot be overstated. Leveraging local support ensured that US-led forces would be welcomed and helped sustain a calm political atmosphere in Somalia throughout the entire relief effort. UNITAF units tried to build on local leadership and reestablish elements of the Somali National Police—one of the few respected national institutions in the country that was not clan-based. The police force staffed checkpoints throughout Mogadishu and provided crowd control at feeding centers. The local police force provided both security and valuable HUMINT to UNITAF.

In contrast, as the mission in Somalia changed from peacekeeping to peace enforcement during UNOSOM II, the UN failed to develop a full awareness of the local population's disposition and did not obtain adequate intelligence on the adversary's intentions and capabilities. In-depth intelligence gathering could have helped the JFC to predict the proclivities of adversaries, their method of operation, and the way in which they interacted with their environment. For example, a greater commitment to intelligence during UNOSOM II would have uncovered the fact that many militia officers had extensive training from the Soviet military academy in Odessa and from Italian military schools. The JFC underestimated the military capabilities of rival factions, and as a result, UN forces were not adequately prepared for contingency situations.

Intelligence gathering is essential to developing operational awareness in the urban environment. A JFC planning an urban operation should attempt to understand the social norms and political customs that define the urban area. A range of HUMINT sources exists to assist the JFC in developing an understanding of the adversary in relation to the urban area. It may be necessary for a JFC planning a joint urban operation to call upon a variety of nontraditional human sources, such as NGOs, foreign experts, anthropologists, regional specialists, expatriates, civil affairs personnel, and special operations forces, for vital information on the urban area.

SOURCE: *Joint Military Operations Historical Collection*

(2) The geospatial intelligence base for contingency operations (GIBCO) is a gathering of imagery, maps, charts, and geospatial data exploited through web browser technology on digital versatile discs through the Defense Logistics Agency or the GIBCO web site on the Joint Worldwide Intelligence Communications System. The tool provides stand-alone access to vast amounts of geospatial data with broad applications including the capability to become familiar with a foreign environment, develop a battle scene, plan and execute NEOs, contingency operations, urban area missions, as a desk-side reference, as well as provide access to geospatial data where networks or infrastructure are down, have been damaged, or do not exist.

i. In some operations, the threat may be environmental, as in the case of a natural disaster. In others, it may be hunger. In still others, there may not be a direct adversary at the onset of operations, but the potential increases for numerous adversaries to arise as the operation develops. The threat may include organized military units, militia groups, clans or tribes, criminal elements, insurgents, terrorists, political factions, or a combination of two or more. For each potential threat, a determination must be made concerning the operational capabilities, COAs, and intentions.

j. **Open-source intelligence** (OSINT) is important in planning and supporting JUOs. The primary source of OSINT is media (radio, television, newspaper, web sites, etc.). An enormous amount of useful urban information is available from geospatial and infrastructure maps, building blueprints, cultural and historical information, and key leaders. The use of native linguists who possess cultural knowledge to fully exploit foreign language sites on the World Wide Web is one key to obtaining the fullest range of useful OSINT. Anonymous tip lines, "rumor mills," text messaging, and other anonymous ways to pass information can be a source of OSINT.

k. **Counterair Threats.** Urban terrain provides excellent cover and concealment for a variety of adversary weapon systems. The urban environment also affects the employment of antiaircraft weapons, including antiaircraft artillery (AAA), man-portable air defense systems, and surface to air missile systems. Adversary light to medium AAA may be employed from ground sites, from the tops of buildings, or weapons mounted on civilian vehicles. The terrain may limit suppression options. The cluttered environment with lights, fires, and smoke will make threat and target acquisition difficult.

l. **Space Support to Intelligence.** The nature of space-based capabilities makes them an important part of intelligence collection in the urban environment.

(1) Space-based systems have access to denied areas that allow them to conduct ISR activities before, during, and after hostilities without being detected by hostile forces or endangering friendly forces. Hostile forces, however, may be aware of overflight times.

(2) Long-term, repeatable observation by space-based ISR assets allows trending and change detection that are particularly useful in the urban environment.

(a) Space systems may detect disturbances such as buried facilities and construction sites. However, built-up areas are particularly challenging since they may contain many such areas that are part of the city landscape and not related to militarily important sites.

(b) Of particular importance, space systems may be able to provide route and target information for targeting—critical for precision fires.

(c) Space systems may also be able to detect camouflage and aid in assessing adversary movements and operations. However, in urban areas concealment is often provided by buildings and structures themselves and not by camouflage. The movement of civilian traffic and the sheer volume of vehicles can mask adversary movement and make identification difficult.

(d) Space systems may be able to provide warning of hostile acts and reconnaissance against friendly forces, depending on the size and nature of the urban area, but the availability of covered avenues of approach makes that capability problematic.

(e) The ability of space systems to detect, track, assess, and report aircraft and vehicular threats is valuable. Again, the presence of a significant number of civilian aircraft and vehicles may make timely identification a problem.

(f) The physical terrain is complex and crowded, with equipment and movement masked by the huge amount of activity in the urban area making surveillance and reconnaissance more difficult. Space systems have little capability to observe interior or subterranean activity. Because urban areas tend to be communications hubs, SIGINT must be gleaned from the multitude of signals that are not operationally significant. The complex physical terrain, large numbers of civilians working and moving in the urban area, and presence of significant communications, transportation, and other infrastructure can affect the rapid fusion of information to create a complete picture of the operational environment. Because communications are a key part of coordinating operations in an urban environment, space-based SIGINT can be very useful for identifying enemy command centers and their command structure, locating enemy positions, tracking persons of interest, and predicting enemy activities.

m. Pattern analysis and recognition may detect pending events of interest. This will require the use of subject-matter experts and other resources who understand the cultural implications of patterns in both adversaries and civilians within the urban area and the AOI.

n. **Civil Information Management.** Civil information is critical to the JFC's situational awareness and understanding. Civil information is developed from data about civil areas, structures, capabilities, organizations, people, and events that can be fused, processed, and shared to increase interagency, IGO, and NGOs situational awareness.

For more information, see JP 3-57, Civil-Military Operations.

4. **Fires**

a. **General**

(1) Fires play a key role in JUOs. In the case of operations involving combat, the JFC can use fires to shape the operational environment and to engage the adversary, but perhaps the most important use of fires is in the isolation of the urban area or points within the urban area. Precision munitions make attacks on specific urban targets much more feasible and effective although their precision does not reduce or mitigate all risk. Operations such as those in Yugoslavia, Kosovo, and Iraq have made significant use of precision fires. Even if the operation is not likely to involve combat, fires are an essential capability in force protection and should be planned. In urban combat, experience has shown that a strong combined arms capability is necessary for success; fires and maneuver are complementary functions that are essential to achieving JFC objectives.

(2) Even when the joint force employs precision weapons, fires can still adversely affect the achievement of objectives. Fires can cause displacement of the civilian population, destruction of critical infrastructure, alienation of local inhabitants and the international community, and increased determination on the part of the adversary.

For further information, see JP 3-09, Joint Fire Support.

b. **Fires Considerations in Operations Conducted in Urban Environments**

(1) Urban environments present unique considerations for the planning and execution of fires. In an urban environment, both the ability to use fires to support missions and the ability to synchronize and integrate fires are considerably more difficult than in other operations. Direct fires sometimes become the firepower means of choice, and can have operational-level significance. In many environments, restrictive ROE and political constraints may compound these problems. The JFC must consider the potential for collateral damage, the possibility of hazardous material contamination, the effects on the civilian populace, the requirements for critical infrastructure in later phases, and any other possibilities that may affect the achievement of operational and strategic objectives.

(2) The complex physical terrain of urban areas—horizontal and vertical surfaces, interior and exterior space, surface and subsurface areas—can severely limit the ability of joint forces to employ fires. The vertical surfaces of buildings can easily mask targets from surface attack and create urban canyons that diminish air capabilities and can cause high and turbulent winds that can reduce the accuracy of fires. Height and proximity of surrounding buildings, different types of structures, construction materials, and structural density all may have an adverse effect on fires. Interior and subterranean spaces offer an adversary positions that are both difficult to locate and hard to reach. Damage caused by combat can create even more protection as rubbled areas may offer defensive advantages. The clutter of closely spaced structures can also adversely affect targeting and assessment. Communications difficulties caused by urban terrain can interfere with effective fire support and control. The characteristics of some weapons make them less suitable in urban terrain than in other areas.

(3) The presence of large numbers of civilians can also severely inhibit the use of fires. There is a real potential for tactical events to have operational- or strategic-level implications—particularly events such as civilian casualties or damaged infrastructure. Since most JUOs will include constraints designed to minimize civilian casualties, the joint force will be required to use fires accordingly. These measures can take several forms: prohibiting attacks on targets located in heavily populated areas, restricting munitions used in attacks, restricting attacks to certain times of the day, giving warning prior to attacks so that civilians can evacuate the area, and aborting attacks unless accuracy can be guaranteed.

(4) Preservation of infrastructure is a concern during planning and execution of JUOs. The presence of critical infrastructure is common in urban areas and, depending on the operational objectives, the JFC may need either to preserve all infrastructure, render selected infrastructure temporarily unusable, or destroy some or all. In addition, urban areas probably contain a number of culturally significant sites that are also likely to have a

protected status. In any case, the presence of significant infrastructure and protected sites increases the requirements for accurate identification and targeting, precise delivery of fires, and concern for collateral damage.

(5) **Combat assessment** includes battle damage assessment (BDA) on operational targets, munitions effectiveness assessment (MEA), and reattack recommendations. Assessment of munitions effectiveness is difficult in urban areas, but an on-the-ground assessment can reveal different types of construction, materials used, structural dimensions, and other aspects of man-made construction that may affect weapons effectiveness.

(6) **Nonlethal Effects.** Creating nonlethal effects during urban operations is important due to limitations imposed on using lethal fires and greater public sensitivity to military and civilian casualties. JFCs seek options to mitigate collateral damage and minimize civilian casualties, particularly in heavily populated areas. Nonlethal effects can be used to incapacitate, suppress, deny access, and move targeted personnel, and to stop or disable materiel while minimizing fatalities, permanent injury, and undesired damage to property in the target area.

(a) Employment of nonlethal capabilities must be integrated into operations to produce synergistic results. Examples are obscuration smoke, illumination fire to disrupt enemy activity or support friendly forces, electric muscular incapacitation devices, and employment of some information-related capabilities, such as electronic attack and offensive cyberspace operations, that deceive the enemy, disable the enemy's C2 systems, and disrupt enemy operations. But the employment of nonlethal effects in supporting these operations must consider their potential political impact as well as the potential for indirect second and third order lethal collateral effects.

(b) Nonlethal weapons and weapons that produce low collateral damage may have greater utility in urban areas. When civilians and hostile forces are intermingled, nonlethal weapons will provide the JFC a broader range of capabilities intended to significantly reduce undesired injuries to civilians and damage to infrastructure. The synergies provided by both lethal and nonlethal force can minimize undesired casualties and damage to materiel, which reduces the potential for conflict escalation, and eases the burden of post-conflict transition and reconstruction.

(7) **Friendly Fire Prevention Measures.** The very nature of the physical terrain in urban areas creates a situation of reduced visibility, with resultant unique and significant challenges. Commanders must identify and assess situations that increase the risk of friendly fire in urban areas. The primary preventive measures for limiting friendly fire incidents are command emphasis, disciplined operations, close coordination among component commands, rehearsals, reliable CID, effective procedures, and enhanced situational awareness. Detailed grid maps or photos aid in target description and accurate location and ultimately friendly fire prevention. Prior coordination is required to ensure all units, both on the ground and in the air, have the correct charts or imagery.

For further discussion regarding friendly fire mitigation, see JP 3-09.3, Close Air Support.

c. **Targeting**

(1) In order to maximize the effects of fires on the adversary while at the same time minimizing the adverse effects on the city and its inhabitants, fires must be as accurate as technology and planning will allow and synchronized with other operations. **The targeting process must take into consideration all the factors associated with fires and the urban environment when developing target lists, including the law of war, the applicable ROE or RUF, and requirements.** Target development is a combination of art and science. It examines the components and relationships among systems such as military, political, or economic to establish their criticality and vulnerability to attack.

(2) **Characteristics of Targets in Urban Areas**

(a) Although single targets exist, most often a target's significance lies in its relationship to other targets or to a greater system. A group of targets related functionally within a country forms a **target system.** The basis for target development is to identify and analyze target systems and their effects on the adversary's military capabilities. Since the urban area is itself a composite of systems, this approach to target development is appropriate for all targets in urban areas.

(b) Identification of time-sensitive targets (TSTs) is an important consideration for the JFC conducting operations in urban environments. A TST is defined as a JFC-designated target requiring immediate response because it is a highly lucrative, fleeting target of opportunity or it poses (or will soon pose) a danger to friendly forces. The JFC normally provides specific guidance and prioritization for TSTs within the operational area.

(3) **No-Strike and Restricted Target Considerations.** The JFC may prohibit or restrict joint force attacks on specific targets or objects without specific approval based on political considerations, military risk, collateral damage risk, the law of war, and ROE. CA can support the development of a restricted target list with civil information management.

Refer to JP 3-60, Joint Targeting, *for additional information.*

d. **Joint Fire Support**

(1) Because the conduct and coordination of indirect fires in urban areas is difficult, fires in support of operational maneuver must be closely coordinated and planned in detail, to include considerations of weapons effects, psychological effects on the populace, and potential collateral damage. For air-delivered munitions, terminal control and guidance can help ensure the delivering platform has acquired the correct target, thus reducing the risk of friendly fire. Effective airspace control measures can ensure other missions (for example, reconnaissance and strike packages) can simultaneously transit or operate in the airspace above and around the urban area.

(2) **Weapons Effects Considerations.** The effects of weapons and munitions in urban areas can be significantly different from the effects in other environments. The characteristics of the terrain and the nature of urban combat affect both the results and employment of weapons of all types. Specific weapons effects considerations in urban

areas include the type and size of the weapon and round, the construction of the building, and the ability to engage the target.

(3) **CAS.** The complicated urban environment creates unique considerations for planning and conducting CAS operations. These considerations include operations in urban canyons, deconfliction in confined airspace, restrictive ROE, difficulty in threat analysis, the presence of civilians, the potential for collateral damage, and the increased risk of friendly fire. For CAS aircraft, the nature of urban canyons and vertical development may require specific attack headings for ordnance delivery and laser operations. Other urban terrain considerations include, but are not limited to, target acquisition, observation, increased threat to rotary-wing aircraft, and suppression of enemy air defense. Terminal attack control differences in urban terrain include marking tools, proficiency, navigation, gridded reference graphics, LOS communication, urban talk-on, ground unit control measures, and weapons selection.

Refer to JP 3-09.3, Close Air Support, *for additional information.*

e. **Interdiction** is a crucial step in isolating the urban area. Interdiction is an action to divert, disrupt, delay, or destroy an enemy's military surface capability before it can be used effectively against friendly forces, or to otherwise achieve objectives. Interdiction can divert adversary forces intended for urban combat, disrupt C2, communications, intelligence and other systems and capabilities, and delay or destroy forces and supplies. Fires and/or maneuver can be used to interdict. Interdiction operations in urban areas can be problematic and require special considerations. Weather effects caused by the urban environment include increased pollution and aerosols affecting target detection, warmer temperatures affecting infrared signatures, and variable wind speeds and directions affected by building layout. The axis of attack and target designation require extra attention; the problem may be similar to attacking enemy forces in steep mountainous terrain. Larger urban areas with more vertically developed buildings add increased target elevation issues to the targeting problem, and the combination of tall buildings and narrow streets can cause an urban canyon effect leading to masking issues for LOS munitions and targeting sensors. Munitions effects will vary greatly depending on whether the enemy can be attacked in the open versus inside buildings. It requires great care to choose the correct delivery method and munition and fusing option when employing fires in an urban environment.

For additional guidance on interdiction, refer to JP 3-03, Joint Interdiction.

f. **IO.** IO capitalize on the growing sophistication, connectivity, and reliance on information technology as well as the human factors associated with every JUO. IO are a means to shape the operational environment and also a tool to engage the adversary by selectively targeting infrastructure and weapons systems. The IO cell should include representatives of those elements or agencies specifically concerned with the urban aspects of the operation or campaign. Intelligence support is critical to the planning, execution, and assessment of IO. Intelligence support to IO includes the intelligence specific to the urban area concerned.

For further information on IO, see JP 3-13, Information Operations.

(1) **General IO Considerations in JUOs.** IO can affect both civilians and infrastructure. Leadership may include not only military leadership, but civilian political, social, and cultural leadership as well. Urban infrastructure may include communications and information, transportation and distribution, energy, economics and commerce, and administration and human services. All of these are most likely to be located in an urban area. Also located in the same urban areas are the means to influence them—communication channels, cultural and societal organizations, political headquarters, and concentrated popular opinion. Even when JUOs are but part of a larger operation or campaign, many of the targets of IO will be located in urban areas.

(a) Enlist influential local indigenous authorities to communicate key information to the population. Efforts should be taken to ensure that association with US forces does not compromise the credibility of these local authorities.

(b) All enemy violations of the law of war can be used to shape local and international opinions. When possible, these violations should be captured on video, distributed to media outlets, and incorporated into the joint force's own MISO. Just as the media will cover adversarial violations, they will cover joint force violations. All joint force members should be alert as to their actions and the potential consequences regardless of who may be watching.

(c) Following enemy attacks, the civilian population may fear direct reprisal from enemy forces. Under such circumstances, inform the population that only the perpetrators and those who support them are the target of operations, and that efforts will be taken to avoid indiscriminate civilian casualties. Employ local law enforcement authorities and judicial systems in redressing such attacks to the extent possible, thereby acting to restore the rule of law.

(2) **MISO Considerations in Urban Environments.** MISO have a fundamental role in JUOs, where the civilian populace and infrastructure often are as important as adversary forces. MISO can do much to shape the urban operational environment before, during, and after actual engagement. MISO can be used independently of or in conjunction with economic, social, and political activities to limit or preclude the use of military force. MISO may be the predominant application of IO used in JUOs.

(a) The physical terrain of the urban area does not have the adverse effect on MISO as it does for many other activities, since MISO generally depend on open sources to disseminate information. The physical nature of the urban area allows the concentration of people and institutions and may make them easier to reach with MISO.

(b) The civilian populace forms one of the primary audiences of MISO, and the urban area contains large numbers of civilians in a relatively small physical area. However, that density also makes it easier for local, tribal, gang, or other group leaders to counteract joint force MISO efforts. The potential complexity of the civilian populace can make MISO efforts challenging, but this complexity also offers a multitude of options and resources for MISO activities.

(c) The physical and service infrastructure of an urban area may enhance MISO by providing the means to disseminate information throughout the operational area. Existing communications systems—television, radio, computers, newspapers and journals—can provide multiple avenues for MISO that are already used by the civilian populace.

(d) The complexity of the urban area enables changes in opinion or attitude to occur quickly. In addition, a military information support (MIS) activity that is effective for a portion of the target audience may leave another target or segment indifferent or even hostile. Continuous assessment, in coordination with up-to-date intelligence, can reduce the possibility of adverse effects resulting from MIS activities and enable MIS planners to make necessary adjustments.

(e) Fundamental to the planning of urban MISO is an understanding of the urban area—language, urban demographics, ethnicity, customs, culture, economics, politics, religion, local and neighborhood allegiances, issues/grievances, and other characteristics of the target population that can affect the way that MISO are perceived.

(f) MISO can be crucial in undermining adversary will. It takes a formidable willpower to fight the urban battle, especially when the resulting destruction is of one's own city, and MISO should be considered an essential weapon in the commander's arsenal. Support from the local populace can enhance the success of JUOs. Accordingly, MISO can gain support for the joint force while reducing support for adversary forces.

(g) MISO can support all types of operations in urban areas, whether or not they involve the use or threat of force. Urban areas are rich with MISO opportunities and resources.

For additional information, refer to JP 3-13.2, Military Information Support Operations.

(3) **Military Deception Considerations for Urban Environments**

(a) The conditions that make operating in an urban environment so challenging are well suited to facilitating deception. While tactics and techniques of deception remain relatively unchanged, the means utilized for execution may be altered and abetted in function by the urban environment. This relationship between urban terrain and deception has six factors:

1. The scope of deceptions is greater in the urban environment than in any other;

2. The cacophonous "background noise" of urban environments hampers counterdeception capabilities;

3. Cities offer a rich trove of materials with which to conduct deception;

4. Decision making is generally impaired in urban environments relative to other environments;

MILITARY INFORMATION SUPPORT OPERATIONS IN RECENT US OPERATIONS

Haiti—Support of Pre-Hostility Military Information Support Operations (MISO) [Formerly Psychological Operations (PSYOP)]

Operation UPHOLD DEMOCRACY (1994-1995) is an excellent example of effective MISO [PSYOP] being employed before committing US forces. Elements from the 4th PSYOP Group deployed to Washington, DC and worked closely with members of the Joint Staff, Assistant Secretary of Defense (Special Operations and Low Intensity Conflict) and the State Department to construct and execute an integrated and effective strategic and operational MISO [PSYOP] plan. General Henry H. Shelton, Commander of the XVIII Airborne Corps for UPHOLD DEMOCRACY, noted: ". . . it is my belief that the integration of PSYOP early in the planning process was critical to the successful execution of the operation. Long before any American military forces stepped ashore, PSYOP helped us quickly accomplish our political and military objectives by laying the foundation for transition. There is no question PSYOP saved lives, on both sides, during Operation UPHOLD DEMOCRACY. It proved to be the unsung, yet vitally important, factor in this operation—a true force multiplier."

Panama—Support of MISO [PSYOP] During Hostilities

In Operation JUST CAUSE (1989) one of the earliest indicators of MISO [PSYOP] effectiveness was the successful employment of loudspeakers and leaflets in support of US Marines at La Chorrera, a small village on the outskirts of Panama City and Howard Air Force Base. The Marines encountered heavy resistance from the Panamanian Defense Force and Dignity Battalion members for the first 24 hours and ceased fire for the night. Surrender appeals were then blared over loudspeakers as safe passage leaflets were dropped. Resistance ceased early the next morning without an additional shot being fired. Surrendering personnel came forward clenching the safe conduct passes.

Bosnia—Support of MISO [PSYOP] During Post-Hostilities

Military information support [PSYOP] forces played a key role during Operation JOINT ENDEAVOR (1995-1996), as part of the North Atlantic Treaty Organization-led Implementation Force in Bosnia-Herzegovina. After the conflict in Bosnia ended, many rural sections were abandoned and the numerous cities and towns in the country were swollen with displaced persons.

Military information support [PSYOP] forces were instrumental in helping to start the US Department of State-sponsored Open Broadcast Network, an alternative daily television venue for the people of Bosnia. In addition, Robert Frowick, the head of the Organization for Security and Cooperation in Europe Bosnian mission, overseeing the Bosnian national elections in 1996, credited the actions by military information support [PSYOP] forces in helping ensure the elections were peaceful and successfully administered.

Iraq—The Second Battle of Fallujah

Weeks ahead of the fight, shaping the operational environment included dropping leaflets inside the city with psychological messages and messages from the Prime Minister to the people of Fallujah. It was clear that if the intimidators were not turned in or if they did not leave the city of their own volition, the Prime Minister would not tolerate the situation in Fallujah.

The leaflets also told the people what was being "stolen" from them by the intimidators—projects to improve the city's sewage, water and schools that could not be initiated as long as thugs dominated the city. They were also told when the attack was coming, so they could leave the city, which really helped limit civilian injuries, keeping them down to almost zero.

Various Sources

<u>5.</u> The presence and proximity of civilians complicate the intelligence picture at all levels;

<u>6.</u> Urban clutter attenuates the leverage of technology.

(b) The above six factors represent a considerable hindrance when facing adversary deception in urban areas, but also create opportunities for US forces conducting JUOs themselves. Historically, deception has offered considerable leverage during operations in an urban environment. It may be both an enhancement to traditional military operations as well as an alternative to them. Although deception is recognized and respected as a potential source of great advantage for adversaries, it has been undervalued as a tool for friendly forces as it is often viewed as an ancillary activity. Deception may exploit technology, but it does not always have to depend on it, thus presenting a capability for JUOs in both high- and low-technology contexts.

(c) Deception applies to urban combat operations no less than elsewhere. Consider its employment to turn enemy forces out of their determined positions or cause them to concentrate, among other potential uses.

For additional information, refer to JP 3-13.4, Military Deception.

g. **Limiting Collateral Damage.** The inadvertent or secondary damage occurring as a result of actions initiated by friendly or adversary forces is a consideration when delivering fires. Choosing an appropriate weapons system, munition warhead, warhead fuzing, and final attack axis are all methods used to mitigate collateral damage.

For further information on mitigating collateral damage, see JP 3-60, Joint Targeting, *and Chairman of the Joint Chiefs of Staff Instruction (CJCSI) 3160.01,* No-Strike and The Collateral Damage Estimation Methodology (U).

SARAJEVO—MINIMIZING COLLATERAL DAMAGE

The focus of the international media was so concentrated in Sarajevo that the Commander in Chief [Allied Forces, South] stated, "Every bomb was a political bomb." If Serbian forces had the opportunity to exploit public opinion in a manner that influenced diplomatic efforts, the military's credibility and support could have suffered. Accordingly, the intent was to preserve as much of the infrastructure of Sarajevo as possible, while destroying the military foundations of Serbian power. To this end, the North Atlantic Treaty Organization (NATO) employed precision-guided munitions during air strikes to minimize collateral damage. The minimal collateral damage resulting from air strikes relieved political pressure on NATO, and NATO was able to sustain the intensity of the operation and increase pressure on the Bosnian Serbs to negotiate a diplomatic settlement to the conflict.

SOURCE: *Joint Military Operations Historical Collection*

5. Movement and Maneuver

a. **General.** Operational movement and maneuver allow the JFC to engage the adversary on terms most favorable to friendly forces. Once the decision has been made to conduct operations in urban areas, movement can range from efforts to position forces to best conduct forcible entry into an urban area to advantageous positioning in preparation for an operation unlikely to involve combat.

b. **Movement and Maneuver Considerations in Urban Environments**

(1) The physical terrain of most urban areas makes the movement of large forces difficult, even in times of peace and stability. In situations of turmoil, the difficulties are magnified. The patterns of streets and structures can be confusing to navigate, tend to break up large formations or canalize them toward city centers, are easily interdicted by fire, and can be easily turned into obstacles and barriers. Conventional avenues of approach in urban areas—highways, wide thoroughfares, railways, and rivers—are easily blocked or interdicted.

(2) Civilians, by their sheer numbers, can act as an impediment to both movement and maneuver. LOCs and avenues of approach to and from assembly areas may be choked with civilians leaving the urban area. Normal civilian traffic can make it nearly impossible to conduct movement except during certain hours of the day. In urban combat, the presence of civilians will certainly affect the ability to use fires in support of maneuver.

(3) Debarkation and staging areas, such as ports or airfields, may also be located within or close to significantly built-up areas and may themselves be vulnerable to interdiction. Routes to and from ports and airfields often pass through the very densely populated and built up areas the joint force is trying to control. There may be no suitable areas for reception and staging near the debarkation points. Roads, railway lines, and rivers may also offer routes into the urban area, but they are also subject to interdiction and

blockages. Air routes into the urban area may be less prone to obstruction. However, a determined adversary with even rudimentary air defense weapons can impede movement of aircraft. Even if the debarkation points are part of the urban area, commanders should attempt to find a secure area large enough to stage and posture operational forces even when forced entry into the JOA is not expected. The commander should be aware of the effects this influx of joint military force may have on the local population. These effects may be in the form of resentment or anxiety, disruption of normal movement patterns, displacement of port or airfield workers, overburdening of services such as water and electricity, or other disruptions. The JFC should take steps to lessen any adverse effects among the civilian populace during this initial deployment of forces. The infrastructure required for debarkation and movement within the JOA may require improvement or restoration before it can be fully utilized. Port facilities, runways, and roads may be inadequate for the movement of forces and may require the early deployment of assets capable of making the necessary modifications to enable full deployment to occur.

(4) The local infrastructure may be insufficient for the introduction of joint forces and may require substantial improvement before being fully usable. Infrastructure considerations such as dependable electric power, water, and sanitation may also affect the movement of forces into the urban area. For operational maneuver, the quality of the transportation system within the urban area can be key to the joint force's ability to maneuver. Adversaries with knowledge of the transportation system—roads, subways, utility tunnels, alleys, sewers, and other routes—can both enhance their ability to maneuver and prevent friendly maneuver from achieving its objectives.

(5) Posturing and concentrating forces within the urban area may affect the urban environment, particularly civilians. Dismounted maneuver, when feasible, facilitates social contact with the populace and may provide distinct advantages over mounted maneuver.

(6) Forces designated to perform operations in urban areas should move, if possible, to reception and staging areas outside the urban area where they will conduct operations.

(7) Although airmobile operations offer another option for movement and maneuver in urban areas, the close spacing of buildings, narrow streets, and higher turbulent winds in some circumstances, may negate the joint force's ability to conduct these operations. Consequently, the airdrop and airland of personnel, equipment, and supplies may have to be conducted at a staging area outside of the urban area.

(8) **Operations in depth may consist of attacks far beyond the urban area itself, on targets that affect the JUO, or they may take place within or near the urban area itself.** When the urban area itself is the focus of the campaign or major operation, the operational environment is constricted and operational depth may be measured in miles, not hundreds of miles. Even in that case, however, operations in depth may include such distant targets as water supply, power plants, communications relay sites, adversary C2 or assembly areas, or key transportation nodes. Within the urban area, an example of operations in depth could be the simultaneous seizure of key objectives in different parts of the urban area. Such operations may be conducted frequently as forcible entry by land or maritime forces, or SOF.

(9) While all forms of maneuver apply to urban combat, some have greater application than others. The JFC may use ground, air, maritime, cyberspace, and space-based assets to isolate the urban area. In addition, land forces provide the capability to seize important objectives and DPs, to facilitate the removal of civilians, monitor and influence behavior, and conduct systematic sweeps of the urban environment. Air assets can be employed to penetrate an area on multiple axes and rapidly project power. In any urban combat maneuver, the best approach is to use the full range of combined arms technology and weaponry available to the joint force, supported by IO. Figure IV-2 provides examples of operational maneuver in a JUO.

(10) **Maneuver Within the Urban Area.** The urban environment significantly affects the ability of the joint force to maneuver by canalizing, increasing vulnerability, reducing options, and slowing movement. Structures pose obstacles that force movement along streets and block movement between streets, thus canalizing and compartmentalizing units and exposing them to fires. This in turn affects the joint force's ability to change directions, reposition, reinforce, bypass adversary resistance, and/or maneuver to the flank. Buildings and the urban population provide adversary cover and concealment and increase the vulnerability of the maneuvering forces, whether land or air. The nature of urban terrain slows maneuver, partly because of the barriers and obstacles either already present or created during operations and because of the physical demands of these operations. In addition, the urban defender generally has interior LOCs, allowing defenders to quickly react to maneuver on the part of an attacking force. Coordinated and integrated horizontal and vertical maneuver in the urban area can slow the defender's ability to react and use interior lines.

(a) **Envelopment** inside an urban area can be difficult to accomplish. The density of the adversary force and the physical terrain it occupies may make it difficult to find an exposed surface flank or make an airborne assault impractical. In those cases, it may require a frontal assault to create an assailable flank. Effective employment of air, land, maritime, space, cyberspace, and SOF capabilities can significantly increase the speed of maneuver to exploit the situation. Envelopment in JUOs can be vertical, rather than horizontal, and requires visualization and planning in three dimensions.

(b) A **turning movement** typically requires greater depth than other forms of maneuver. The required depth may not be available in an urban area.

(c) **Infiltration** depends on situational awareness and understanding of the urban area, careful selection of objectives, detailed planning, and efficient support and deception. Infiltration is not likely to be attempted by large conventional forces, but rather small units. A hostile civilian population reduces the prospects for success.

(d) **Penetration** requires surprise and careful planning. Care must be taken to secure the flanks of the penetrating force.

(e) During combat operations in urban areas, **frontal assault** by land forces may be inevitable. The joint force's chances of success in executing this form of maneuver can be greatly enhanced by its ability to apply overwhelming combat power against specific objectives with rapid maneuver and precision fires.

Examples of Operational Maneuver

Envelopment

- The Israelis struck to the east of Beirut during the 1982 Operation PEACE FOR GALILEE, linking up with the Christian militias and severing the Beirut-Damascus road, thereby cutting off all supply and reinforcement to the Palestine Liberation Organization.

- During the Summer 1942 offensives on the Eastern Front, German forces enveloped the heavily defended fortress city of Sevastopol by land, sea, and air, isolating it from Soviet reinforcements. Despite difficult terrain, determined military and civilian defenders, and rough parity in ground forces, the Germans were able to secure the town.

Turning Movement

- Operation CHROMITE (1950) uncovered Seoul and caused the headlong retreat of the North Korean armies.

- The sweep westward during Operation DESERT STORM (1991) forced the Iraqis to abandon Kuwait City without offering a significant resistance.

Infiltration

- In Hue, the North Vietnamese Army quietly infiltrated two regiments and seized most of the city in a single day (1968).

- In Operation JUST CAUSE (1989), units were staged unnoticed at bases throughout Panama and special operations forces infiltrated key locations. The simultaneous attack on key locations throughout the country made adversary response weak and disjointed.

Penetration

- After crossing the Suez Canal in 1973, the Israeli Defense Force (IDF) attempted a quick armored penetration to seize Suez City. Egyptian regular and irregular forces turned back the attack and inflicted heavy losses on IDF units.

- In the initial attack on Grozny in 1994, Russian forces tried a similar armored penetration, with even worse results.

Frontal Attack

- Operational level frontal attacks include the German attack at Stalingrad, the Marines' battle to retake Hue, and the Russian attack on Grozny after the failed penetration.

Figure IV-2. Examples of Operational Maneuver

(11) As difficult as urban maneuver may be, there are several actions the JFC can take to reduce risk and increase the likelihood of success.

(a) **Isolation of the urban area is nearly always a prerequisite for success.** The joint force can cut off or control outside support, information, and influence through air, space, land, maritime, and information superiority by interdiction, physical presence, control of basic services, and control of lines and means of communications. The purpose is to control the flow of supplies, personnel, and information into and within the urban area and to physically and psychologically isolate the area. Within the urban area itself, isolation of selected areas may be a prerequisite for controlling them. The JFC should consider both the beneficial and detrimental effects of such control and isolation on the civilian populace.

(b) **Combined arms organization ensures that forces have all the elements at hand to conduct operations in urban environments.** The difference between the makeup of combined arms organizations needed for operations in urban areas and operations conducted in other environments is the proportion and organizational level of different types of forces. For example, armored forces may not be required in the same strength and organization as in operations in open country, while the need for engineer capability increases. The sometimes-accepted presumption that tracked vehicles are undesirable during JUOs has repeatedly proven false; however, a mix of tracked and wheeled armored vehicles is often appropriate. Thermal sights on armored vehicles can be used effectively to locate enemy units hiding in buildings.

(12) The JFC may employ unexpected maneuver. The early seizure of key operational objectives by penetration can facilitate control of the populace and local infrastructure. Shows of force throughout the urban area can discourage resistance.

(13) It may be necessary to conduct **defensive operations** in urban areas, either to deny the adversary strategic or operational objectives, to retain a key economic or political center, to control LOCs and avenues of advance, or for reasons of economy of force. Operational considerations in urban defense mirror those of offensive operations: the purpose of the defense; the degree of delay and denial desired; impact on civilians; acceptable friendly casualties; the type of defense; whether to defend inside or outside the city; whether to defend the entire urban area, a key sector, or COG; and the amount of physical destruction anticipated and allowable.

(14) The JFC must counteract the impact of natural and man-made barriers, obstacles, and mines. In JUOs, these may include ports and airfields and their approaches, transportation systems (roads, railroads, and canals), natural formations such as mountains or rivers, minefields, risks from industrial and CBRN hazards, and even highly congested sections of the urban area itself. **In order to overcome urban barriers and obstacles and provide operational mobility, the JFC may have to employ substantial engineering or other support assets** immediately after initial seizure of the immediate area around the barrier or obstacle. Sea mines and some land minefields can be cleared prior to the introduction of land forces, but other barriers and obstacles require hands-on preparation, restoration, or improvement. These actions can be more difficult in urban areas because of the difficulty in securing areas dominated by vertical structures or natural terrain, and a substantial investment in forces may be necessary to protect the mobility effort.

(15) **Operational countermobility** can be achieved by the employment of operational obstacles, the institution of embargo or blockade, or by maritime interdiction. In JUOs, any and all of these methods may be pertinent. Defense of an urban area in itself can constitute the employment of a system of obstacles. Joint forces can create urban obstacles in a number of ways: enhance natural or man-made choke points, destroy bridges and tunnels, establish minefields, or create other obstacles.

For more information, see JP 3-15, Barriers, Obstacles, and Mine Warfare for Joint Operations.

(16) The JFC may take steps to dominate or control those aspects of the urban environment whose possession or control provides either side with an operational advantage. Denial of an operational area can be accomplished either by occupying the key area itself or by limiting use or access to the area. For an area, critical factor, or function to be operationally key, its dominance or control must achieve operational or strategic results or deny the same to the adversary. In JUOs, the key areas, critical factor, or function may be approaches to the urban area, dominating physical terrain and airspace within or near the urban area, man-made features important to the success of the operation, or nonphysical activities such as the social, cultural, economic, or political. The joint force can dominate or control an operationally significant land area by physical occupation, through fire, or through the threat of fires. It may be possible to dominate other key urban areas without entering the urban area, by entering only in selected places, or by attacking critical targets. Sustained domination of key urban areas, though, normally requires either physical occupation or physical destruction.

6. Protection

a. **General. Although protection will not ensure the success of operations in urban areas, failure to take adequate protection measures can cause an operation to fail.** The protection function focuses on conserving the joint force's fighting potential in four primary ways—active defensive measures that protect the joint force (including DOD civilians and DOD contractors), its information, its bases, necessary infrastructure, and LOCs from an adversary's attack; passive defensive measures that make friendly forces, systems, and facilities difficult to locate, strike, and destroy; applying technology and procedures to reduce the risk of friendly fire; and emergency management and response to reduce the loss of personnel and capabilities due to accidents, health threats, and natural disasters.

b. **Protection Considerations in Urban Environments**

(1) The physical urban terrain makes protection difficult in many ways. The vertical terrain means that observation of friendly formations, movement, and bases is easier. It becomes difficult to secure LOCs, joint security areas, bases, and installations when they are easily observed and interdicted. Dispersion within the urban area means that more sites and nodes may require hardening and defense. Threats can be vertical rather than horizontal, and require visualization in three dimensions. The compartmented, three-dimensional nature of urban terrain places a premium on all-around security. Units that do not heed this stricture often find themselves attacked from the rear or from above.

See JP 3-10, Joint Security Operations in Theater, *for additional discussion of joint security operations.*

(2) Civilians pose an even more severe challenge. Their large numbers and presence in all parts of the urban area make operations security challenging. Adversaries may use civilians as camouflage, shields, and even targets. Their presence inhibits protective fires and adds to the difficulty of evasion and PR. The effects of attacks using WMD, terrorism, or conventional attacks on friendly forces are magnified by the presence of civilians. Their suffering, even when minimized, can have operational and strategic

consequences. Use of nonlethal capabilities can serve to assist friendly forces in differentiating between civilians and hostiles using civilians as human shields. By using nonlethal weapons to separate hostile forces from civilians, the effectiveness of lethal fires may be enhanced while avoiding undue civilian casualties or collateral damage.

(3) Existing infrastructure can aid in the protection of the force. However, local infrastructure —when used by the force—may become a protection responsibility that can be more difficult than military infrastructure. Civilian buildings, such as communications facilities, are more difficult to defend and secure. The often large and sprawling nature of water systems, power plants, transportation systems, and government buildings make their protection a challenging proposition. Communications security and electronics security should consider the presence and potential use of local communications and electromagnetic radiation.

(4) The urban environment offers a unique set of actual or potential hazardous conditions. The JFC must **identify** hazards, actual or potential, that can result in injury, illness, or death to personnel or civilians, damage to equipment, property, or infrastructure, or any other condition that can degrade the mission.

(5) To assess the identified hazards in terms of probability and severity, the JFC must have an accurate understanding of the threat, the urban area itself, and the current conditions within the urban area. The JFC can then determine the risk level of each identified hazard or condition that can adversely affect the achievement of operational or strategic objectives, either directly or through branches or sequels. When an urban hazard exists, such as use or threat of use of WMD by a terrorist, with potentially catastrophic effects on operations, the commander is alerted to take protection measures against it. A sniper attack on friendly and multinational personnel in the urban area may only marginally degrade operational capability, but since its likelihood is judged to be frequent, again the commander is obliged to take preventive measures.

(6) Based on the assessment of hazards in the urban area, the JFC develops controls to either eliminate the hazard or reduce the risk. Some hazards can be partially controlled by a thorough understanding of the urban area. Other controls may take the form of barriers and defenses, IO, increased security precautions, PRC, personnel rotation, development of response plans and capabilities, drills, warning systems, communications, or intelligence. Despite control measures, the residual risk is likely to be high due to the inability to fully control all conditions in such a large and complex area.

(7) **Faced with the superiority of US forces, most adversaries seek an asymmetrical advantage. Urban areas are a natural battleground for insurgents and terrorists: the effects of their acts are greater and more noticeable and the groups themselves more difficult to locate and identify.** Urban areas offer terrorists both a wide range of targets and an environment that facilitates the use of a variety of means and methods of attack (e.g., sabotage, DA with conventional munitions, or attacks using WMD). Targets may include barracks and bases, military movement routes, small units, individual personnel, USG departments and agencies, NGOs, civilian or military infrastructure, or civilians. Friendly and multinational forces are a likely target for terrorist attacks, and remain so.

CHEMICAL, BIOLOGICAL, RADIOLOGICAL, AND NUCLEAR INCIDENT IN AN URBAN AREA

On 2 April 1979, there was an anthrax outbreak which affected 94 people and killed at least 64 of them in the Soviet city of Sverdlovsk, which contained a biological warfare development facility. As it turned out, it was an accidental release, and the wind carried the anthrax away from the city. If the wind had been in the opposite direction that day—toward the city of Sverdlovsk—the death rate could have been in the hundreds of thousands and many facilities would have been contaminated.

Various Sources

Terrorists receive significant operational and strategic results from even a low-level attack. Further adding to the protection problem is the presence of large numbers of civilians and key civilian infrastructure. Attacks on civilians may provide terrorist organizations with similar benefits and less risk than attacks on friendly and multinational forces.

(8) Improvised explosive device (IED) awareness, lessons learned, and counter-IED tactics are an important protection consideration in urban areas.

See JP 3-15.1, Counter-Improvised Explosive Device Operations, *for additional discussion of and lessons learned in counter-IED tactics.*

(9) **Serious consequences occur if adversaries use CBRN weapons in urban areas or if there is a deliberate or accidental release of TIMs.** Expect significant numbers of casualties to civilian populations and to unprotected military forces if adversaries create a CBRN incident in an urban environment. There will be personnel, equipment, and site contamination; dislocated civilians; medical facilities may be overwhelmed; and diseases may spread. It is very difficult to detect release of CBRN before symptoms manifest in the population.

(a) Urban areas often include manufacturing plants, which may be a source of TIMs. An adversary could intentionally target these types of facilities in order to cause destruction and widespread contamination for the force or other people in the urban area. Joint forces may inadvertently strike or damage TIM infrastructure causing serious collateral effects. JFCs must consider the presence of TIM facilities during planning and, if possible, determine the risk and impact of intentional or unintentional release. The industrial accident at Chernobyl's nuclear power plant in April 1986 highlights the potential serious effects of the release of radioactivity upon an urban area. Hundreds of thousands of civilians had to abandon entire cities and settlements within the thirty-kilometer zone of extreme contamination.

(b) Improvised chemical devices can be a threat and JFCs should monitor and possibly control the distribution of industrial or agricultural chemicals that could be used in constructing a chemical explosive device. Other devices the JFC should be aware of are radiological emitting devices, radiological dispersal devices, and improvised nuclear devices.

c. **Security in Urban Environments**

(1) Security in urban environments consists of three main areas, and all involve the security of civilians to some degree.

(a) **Security of the Force.** Force protection is a required task in any operation. In JUOs, where support and protection of civilians is a legal requirement and may be a mission objective, the ability of the force to provide support depends on the security with which it can do so.

(b) **Security of Civilians.** Commanders have an obligation to protect civilians, as combat operations and force protection will allow. In many operations security of civilians is a stated operational objective. These operations may include peacekeeping, combating terrorism, FHA, or FID. Security of civilians may consist of protection from military operations, from terrorism, from opposing groups or factions, or from criminal activity.

(c) **Security of Civilian Agencies.** Governmental agencies, IGOs, and NGOs will operate within the urban area. These civilians, while not part of the local populace, may require various forms of security from the force, ranging from perimeter and point security to armed escort.

(2) **Proactive actions on the part of the force enhance security**, both for civilians and the force itself. These actions include close contact and communications with local civilians and organizations and with other civilian agencies, extensive patrolling, MISO, barrier construction, mine and obstacle clearance, movement control, and provision of needed support. The JFC must avoid complacency in urban areas where the threat may be difficult to identify.

(3) The coastal riverine force can protect strategic port facilities and strategic commercial shipping and naval ships in harbor approaches, at anchorages and in ports, from bare beach to sophisticated port facilities, in order to ensure the uninterrupted flow of cargo and personnel to the JFC. Coastal riverine force operations protect these assets from waterborne and land-based threats.

For more information, refer to Navy Tactics, Techniques, and Procedures (NTTP) 3-06.1, Riverine Operations.

d. **PR.** PR is the sum of military, diplomatic, and civil efforts to prepare for and execute the recovery and reintegration of isolated personnel. Isolated personnel are those US military, DOD civilians and contractor personnel (and others designated by the President or SecDef) who are separated from their unit (as an individual or a group) while participating in a US-sponsored military activity or mission and are, or may be, in a situation where they must survive, evade, resist, or escape.

(1) **Evasion in an Urban Area.** The likelihood of being isolated in an urban area is increasing. With so few available helicopter landing zones and the high vulnerability of recovery vehicles or forces in any given urban area, it is likely that isolated personnel will

need to evade for a substantial amount of time, avoiding observation and contact. The evader must always be ready to fight, if necessary, and travel extended distances to get to a feasible recovery site or friendly forces. Generally, successful evasion in an urban area requires an in-depth knowledge of the local area and attitude of the populace.

(2) PR in urban environments presents unique challenges for commanders during operations. Urban environments also present significant challenges for isolated personnel. Escape and evasion is particularly problematic under urban conditions, depending on the demographic/sociocultural characteristics of the local population and other unique aspects of the urban environment.

(3) In the urban operational environment seizure of personnel through kidnapping/hostage taking for ransom or propaganda purposes can no longer be considered isolated or aberrant acts, but must be regarded as a normal enemy tactic. Because of the significant detrimental effects such incidents can have on morale and public support for the military mission, this tactic and its implications for PR must be recognized as an important consideration when planning operations in urban environments.

(4) Risk mitigation/prevention of seizure of personnel is accomplished through threat-specific operational procedures and properly focused force protection training. Successful PR following a seizure of personnel event is far more likely if the personnel involved are properly organized, trained, equipped, and employed. JFCs are responsible for accomplishing PR execution tasks throughout the operational area. They must consider all available PR options and categories to successfully plan for recovery operations.

For further guidance on PR, refer to JP 3-50, Personnel Recovery, *as well as Joint Personnel Recovery Agency urban evasion documentation available on the classified Joint Personnel Recovery Agency Web site at www.jpra.smil.mil.*

   e. **CID.** CID in urban environments is an important issue for ROE considerations. CID is the process of attaining an accurate characterization of detected objects in the operational environment sufficient to support an engagement decision. Depending on the situation and the operational decisions that must be made, this characterization may be limited to "friend," "enemy," or "neutral." In other situations, other characterizations may be required—including, but not limited to class, type, nationality, and mission configuration. Considerations include:

   (1) How does the urban environment impact visualization of friendly forces?

   (2) How are multinational and indigenous force tracking capabilities integrated?

   (3) How are CID systems and blue force tracking capabilities effectively integrated for effective C2?

   (4) What degree of latency is acceptable for visualization of friendly force locations; real-time or near real-time?

STALINGRAD—THE SPREAD OF AN EPIDEMIC

Already in January 1942, the region that encompasses Stalingrad was experiencing the effects of a tularemia epidemic. 14,000 cases were reported that winter. With the onset of the battle in August 1942, the entire public health system supporting Stalingrad collapsed. The hygiene and sanitation systems were disrupted.

According to one Soviet retrospective: in the fall of 1942 at the height of the battle, "more than 75 percent of the population was hit by tularemia in individual locations of the Stalingrad area. As the health centers were practically out of order, the entire burden of the treatment of the infected population was taken up by the military medical front service."

Exacerbating the epidemic was that the fighting had disrupted the harvest activities in the area. Crops were not harvested, which provided a large source of food for the resultant explosion in the rodent population. Rodents were a disease vector for the spread of the epidemic, as were mosquitoes and by inhalation. Tularemia infected rodents got into everything (bedding, food, water), and affected the fighting capacity of both armies.

After the battle, the number of cases of tularemia returned to pre-battle levels.

SOURCE: Eric Croddy, MA, Tularemia, Biological Warfare
and the Battle of Stalingrad 1942-43, an editorial from
Military Medicine, Vol. 166, No. 10, October 2001

f. **Force health protection (FHP)** complements force protection efforts and includes all measures taken by the JFC and the Military Health System to promote, improve, and conserve the mental and physical well-being of Service members. FHP measures focus on the prevention of illness and injury. Breakdown in urban hygiene and sanitation systems, as well as disruption to the area's area food supply, may contribute to localized or widespread outbreaks of famine, disease, and infections, especially if the region is already experiencing a natural, periodic epidemic. The JFC must ensure adequate capabilities are available to identify health threats and implement appropriate FHP measures. Health threats arise from potential and ongoing enemy actions to include employment of CBRN threats and hazards; environmental, occupational, industrial, and meteorological conditions; endemic human and zoonotic diseases; and other medical considerations that can reduce the effectiveness of military forces. Therefore, a robust health surveillance system is critical to FHP measures.

For further guidance on FHP, refer to JP 4-02, Health Services.

7. **Sustainment**

a. **General.** The nature of operations in urban environments creates unique support demands. Increased densities but the potential for greater dispersion may mean more nodes to supply, maintain, and support. The quantities of supplies required will differ from other types of operations, as will the types and amount of medical services required. Forces will need reconstitution more frequently. All movement will entail more risk and be more difficult to accomplish. Navigation and communications will be more difficult. Map accuracy may be insufficient for navigation and calls for fire. Landmarks may be destroyed, signs missing or deliberately altered. GPS signals will suffer interruptions. Night operations may be favored, but this will make navigation even more difficult. Spellings may differ on various maps and signs. Sustaining bases may not be possible, or may be difficult to secure. Support requirements to HN and civilian agencies will likely be much greater than in other operations, and may be the focus of the JUO itself. Commanders should consider the way the urban area affects the conduct of service support functions, particularly when those functions are located or performed within an urban area. **Operations in urban areas normally will require more of many types of resources (e.g., personnel, munitions, subsistence, medical support) than other operations.** Commanders must make every effort to anticipate and specifically plan for these resources. It is important for the JFC to clearly specify appropriate supporting and supported relationships to ensure that subordinate commanders conducting JUOs will have sufficient forces and means. The JFC may also need to task organize forces in innovative formations depending on the characteristics of the urban area and the operational objectives. In order to preclude stripping other theater forces of assets required for JUOs, the JFC should identify early in planning those capabilities required from supporting commands. Support activities will play a large role in the transition phase of operations conducted in urban areas.

b. **Sustainment Considerations in Urban Environments**

(1) The complex physical geography of urban areas can have significant effects on support. The close spacing of buildings and streets can affect distribution. There may not be large spaces available for bases. The need to operate in buildings, on streets, and in sewers offers a variety of medical challenges. Communications will be difficult due to blocked signals by buildings and metal structures in the area. Personnel operating in urban areas will be exposed to electrical and fire hazards from downed power lines, fuel leaks, and industrial chemical spills and contamination. Urban terrain can have restrictive natural terrain features such as rivers as well as narrow roads and closely built structures that impede distribution. Urban areas present an additional vertical dimension that may require operations and sustainment of personnel in multistory buildings and structures that create additional hazards and security considerations.

(2) The presence of large numbers of civilians can easily affect the ability to support joint forces. Sickness and injury can burden medical services. Crowds and congestion can inhibit vehicular movement. The sheer numbers can drain the support capability of the joint force if not considered beforehand.

(3) Infrastructure can help or hinder sustainment operations. Existing services may be able to support the joint force to some extent, but it is more likely that the joint force will need to support local services, to include food and water, health service, transportation management, and utilities. The densely packed civilian population may present myriad mouths to feed or patients to support. Transportation, medical, and other unit types can be overwhelmed. Local government can be of assistance in the contracting of services and supplies, but may be too ineffective to help in a meaningful way. The failure of basic

services can place on the joint force the burden for providing them. The presence of a capable local infrastructure means that the joint force must only support itself, but the likelihood in JUOs is that such infrastructure will not be available. Local infrastructure will likely either be incapable of fully meeting the demands of the population or absent altogether. Because of this, any JUO will probably see a significant presence of NGOs and IGOs. It is important that the JFC and staff coordinate fully with these agencies in order to both relieve any potential burden on the joint force and to ensure that the needs of the civilian population are met. The joint force is better able to accomplish its objectives with the active and efficient cooperation of NGOs and IGOs.

(4) Historically in urban combat operations, ammunition expenditures (particularly for small-arms ammunition) increase dramatically. On the other hand, fuel requirements for operations conducted in urban areas are often less than for operations in open terrain. These different usage rates are an important logistic consideration.

(5) The JFC's responsibility for **equipment maintenance** in the JOA usually entails the establishment of facilities in joint security areas or offshore aboard the sea base for the repair and replacement of materiel. In JUOs, the establishment of such facilities may not be feasible if there is no joint security area or any area large enough for the repair of major items. In urban combat, it is difficult to evacuate damaged equipment, and in a constantly shifting urban battle, there may be no secure routes to maintenance facilities. Maintenance service providers may be forced to come to the equipment rather than have the equipment come to them. In urban combat, it is often easier to replace than to repair, and planners should allow for increased replacement of what might normally be repairable equipment. Maintenance may encompass the full range of vehicles, equipment, and personal gear. Vehicle maintenance must be done quickly as stopped or immobile vehicles can block urban arteries. Engineer capabilities such as bulldozers may be needed to clear damaged vehicles. Maintenance may be performed while exposed to hostile fire. Transport time to deliver spare parts for maintenance may be longer despite the shorter distances to travel.

(6) The intense fighting, coupled with the high casualty rates normally associated with urban combat, often means units can only last a few hours before needing relief. This makes it necessary to pull units back for rest and reconstitution far more frequently than in other types of operations.

(7) Personal clothing and equipment will need replacement on a regular and frequent basis. Tactical units will desire special urban equipment and capabilities such as knee and elbow pads, ropes, goggles, gloves, small-unit radios and batteries, thermal sights, ladders, breaching tools, military working dog teams, robots, biometric identification, nonlethal weapons, and others.

(8) Friendly and multinational forces will be at risk from a wide variety of endemic diseases. Environmental and industrial hazards may pose a threat to deployed forces. A health services plan should include a medical surveillance program, the establishment of a joint patient movement requirements center, and the activation of the JTF joint blood program office.

PSYCHOLOGICAL CASUALTIES IN BEIRUT AND GROZNY

Recent urban conflicts suggest that the psychological casualty rates are much higher in urban operations than in other types. The tempo and experience of urban operations is so intense that soldiers tend to "burn out" quickly.

After-action assessments of Israeli Defense Force (IDF) performance during urban operations during the 1982 Lebanon war point out the difficulty the IDF had sustaining combat operations because of the high stress level urban combat imposed on individual soldiers. This observation is borne out by Israeli casualty figures: 10-24 percent of Israeli soldiers serving in Lebanon experienced psychological problems as a result of their battle experience. This, compared with a psychological casualty rate of only 3.5 percent to 5 percent in the 1973 war means that combat stress casualties suffered in Lebanon were two to five times more serious.

After Russia's 1994-1996 conflict with Chechnya, one medical survey found 72 percent of the soldiers screened had some sort of psychological disorder symptoms. Further, 46 percent of the soldiers exhibited asthenic depression (a weak, apathetic, or retarded motor state) and the other 26 percent exhibited psychotic reactions such as high states of anxiety, excitement or aggressiveness, and a deterioration of moral values or interpersonal relations. The statistics also revealed that the percentage of troops with combat stress disorders was higher than experienced during their 1980s war in Afghanistan. One of the primary differences was that, in Chechnya, Russian forces conducted combat mostly in cities rather than in mountains, valleys, and other rural areas.

SOURCE: Marine Corps Intelligence Activity: *Urban Warfare Study: City Case Studies Compilation*

(a) As previously indicated, urban combat produces high casualties. Because of the high concentration of people and often poor sanitation, urban areas have the strong potential for the outbreak of disease among joint forces. More robust health services will be required for all JUOs, but particularly for those involving combat.

(b) Infectious diseases pose one of the greatest threats in JUOs. Planning for dealing with large numbers of civilians (and casualties) should include measures to protect friendly forces in the JOA from communicable diseases. Proper sanitation and preventive medicine, including animal, rodent, and pest control, should be considered.

(c) Combat stress reactions are magnified in urban combat and require effective psychological prevention and management. Urban combat is mentally, physically, and emotionally exhausting, and the psychological effects on all participants (including health care personnel) can be devastating. While rapid treatment and/or removal from the combat area can often enable combatants to quickly return to duty, it may be more difficult to take these actions with scarce medical personnel. JFCs must plan for the timely recognition and treatment of psychological casualties among both combatants and health care personnel and arrange for replacement of affected personnel.

(d) The physical terrain of urban areas may preclude vehicular or aerial evacuation of casualties. Consequently, units may require more litter bearers to move casualties to collection points where they can be further evacuated by ground or air transport. Lengthy evacuation routes will increase the number of litter bearers required due to fatigue, so commanders may need to augment combat units with additional personnel to perform evacuation. Commanders and staff at all echelons must develop detailed medical evacuation plans, to include engineer support to clear routes for medical evacuation. The compartmented nature of the urban environment, transportation restrictions, communications difficulties, and the finite number of combat medics increases the demand for self-aid and buddy aid. Commanders should plan and train their units accordingly.

(e) Civilian medical facilities that joint forces can use may be present in the urban area. However, it is likely that these facilities will not have the required capabilities to meet the medical needs of the local population. The joint force should include sufficient organic medical capability to treat its wounded, sick, and injured and either return them to duty or evacuate them from the theater or JOA.

(9) Other support areas have particular requirements:

(a) When local capabilities or operations of port or air facilities are insufficient, the JFC provides that capability. There also may exist a need to expand the capabilities of these ports of debarkation early in the deployment process. The JFC may also need to provide rail and road management and control within and perhaps outside the urban area itself in order to ensure efficient movement.

(b) **Basing and Sustainment.** Sustainment activities for JUOs should be located close enough to the urban area to ensure provision of adequate support. Yet, if they are located within the urban area, they are subject to actions by the adversary and the local populace and to the difficulties inherent in the urban infrastructure. There may not be a single area that can house a complete base, and it may be necessary to construct smaller bases for specific types of support. Engineer reconnaissance, geospatial engineering, and early involvement of the joint force engineer are crucial to this element of mission planning.

(c) The requirement to provide **law enforcement** and detainee operations can range from support only for the joint force to extensive support to the local government and populace. An increasingly likely scenario for a JUO is one in which local law enforcement is ineffective, and criminal elements pose a threat to the HN or the joint force. Significant law enforcement support may be required.

See JP 3-63, Detainee Operations, *for more information on the conduct of detainee operations.*

(10) In some JUOs, the largest single operational task is the requirement to provide **support to other nations, groups, and agencies.** Actions in this area may include

providing transportation support, security assistance to the HN, CMO, and interagency support and coordination to transition to civil administration.

c. **Logistic Support to Civilians**

(1) In JUOs, logistic elements may be employed in nonstandard tasks and in quantities disproportionate to their normal military roles. Part of the reason for this is the demands JUOs put on certain types of logistic support. Another factor is the concentration of civilians also requiring support. Logistic elements may have to support both military operations and civilians. They may precede other military units or be the only forces deployed, or they may have continuing responsibility after the departure of combat forces in support of multinational forces or NGOs and IGOs.

(2) **Logistic support to civilians will fall into one of four categories.** It may comprise more than one, or even all, depending on the mission and the situation. This support is limited by applicable laws and regulations, and consultation with Service legal personnel is critical to assure compliance. These categories are as follows:

(a) **Support directly to civilians,** such as the provision of food, water, shelter, and medical treatment.

(b) **Support that indirectly benefits civilians,** such as the restoration of basic infrastructure and services.

(c) **Support to military and government organizations dealing with civilians,** such as support of multinational forces, diplomatic missions, or government agencies.

(d) **Support to HN, NGOs, and IGOs,** such as construction, warehousing, and distribution of supplies.

(3) The density of civilians is a significant influence on logistic support. In JUOs, the concentration of civilians can add a considerable support requirement. Provision of support to civilians may be the primary focus of the operation. **All core logistic functions— supply, maintenance operations, deployment and distribution, health services, engineering, logistic services, and operational contract support—are likely to be taxed to support civilians in JUOs.** The deployment and distribution capability supports the movement of forces and unit equipment during the movement phase of the deployment and redeployment processes, and supports materiel movement during the logistical sustainment of operations. Other services will probably include above-average requirements for such capabilities as waste disposal, contracting, mortuary services, and civil administration, to name a few.

(4) Increased outsourcing of joint logistics must be recognized. The civil augmentation programs (e.g., logistics civil augmentation program, Air Force contract augmentation program) and properly integrating contingency contractors authorized to accompany the force can significantly impact JUOs.

d. Medical Support to Civilians

(1) The health services mission is to conserve the fighting strength of the joint force and to provide the JFC with a source of trained manpower. For combat operations, health services focuses primarily on the treatment and evacuation of wounded and injured and the prevention and treatment of disease. The presence of large numbers of civilians, however, will probably require health services units also to support the civilian populace to some degree in all JUOs within the limits of applicable laws and regulations. Assistance may be required at the same time as health services for the engaged force.

(2) In urban areas, joint force medical units will likely not have primary health services responsibility, but will focus on furnishing assistance to the populace that the local government is not capable of providing. Local medical services may be nonexistent, or at least unable to provide sufficient care for the sick and injured. Relief agencies may or may not be able to alleviate the situation. Military health services may be the only source of medical relief for civilians until other agencies and organizations are functioning. This assistance normally requires a great deal of interaction with HN services and authorities, government agencies, NGOs, and IGOs.

For additional information on working with nonmilitary agencies, refer to JP 3-08, Interorganizational Coordination During Joint Operations, *and JP 4-02,* Health Services.

(3) The health threat to civilians in urban areas is a combination of injuries resulting from combat (including terrorism), injuries and disease occurring naturally, or lack of safe food and water. Because of the density of the population, civilian casualties will occur more frequently and in greater numbers than in other operational environments: weapons effects will injure more civilians; poor sanitation is more likely to cause endemic disease; infectious diseases will spread more quickly.

(4) The JFC should organize health services elements based on the anticipated needs of both the joint force and the civilian populace, within the limits of applicable laws and regulations. Health services representatives should be members of all groups, centers, or teams concerned in any way with the civilian populace, such as the humanitarian assistance survey team, the humanitarian assistance coordination center, or the CMOC. In order to adequately anticipate civilian needs, health service planners must conduct a health service assessment that examines the factors listed in Figure IV-3.

(5) Using the information developed in the health services assessment, the health services plan should consider factors significant to the urban area.

(a) **Intent of the medical support to be provided to civilians.** Is the intent to provide only minimal medical support to the civilian populace, or is nation assistance or FHA a primary mission?

(b) **Special restrictions on the medical care to be provided.** Restrictions may be necessary because of a shortage of medical supplies, cultural considerations, financial or legal constraints, or an attempt to keep the level of care consistent with that normally provided by local health services.

Health Services Assessment Factors

- Population demographics
- Sanitation and personal hygiene
- Endemic diseases
- Available medical intelligence
- Availability and accessibility of health care delivery systems and processes
- Cultural factors related to health services
- Primary care capabilities
- General health of the population

- Political impact of providing care to the local population
- Anticipated type, number, and capabilities of relief organizations
- Secondary and tertiary hospital facilities and supporting transportation
- Local facilities for production of medical equipment and supplies
- Education and training levels of health services professionals and technicians

Figure IV-3. Health Services Assessment Factors

(c) **Most immediate threats in urban area.** Often, regardless of the major event precipitating health services, the most immediate threats will result from extreme environmental conditions in the form of heat, cold, and high humidity.

(d) **Nature and behavior of the particular prevalent diseases.** Communicable diseases spread more rapidly in densely populated urban areas, and any disruption in basic services increases the threat from serious communicable diseases.

(e) **Patient movement.** The need for clear guidance concerning the medical evacuation and treatment of civilians is critical. Unless otherwise specifically authorized by the stated mission, force members will provide only emergency medical services to civilian casualties. Unless otherwise authorized, civilian casualties will be transferred to the nearest available civilian treatment facility when the medical condition is stabilized. While airlift may be available for general patient movement, patients with known or suspected chemical, biological, or radiological contamination or highly contagious diseases will not be transported within the patient movement system by large frame transport aircraft prior to decontamination. See US Transportation Command policy on the transportation of contaminated cargo and personnel.

(f) **Required preventive medicine measures.** Provision of safe water and food, immunizations, and prophylactic medications can reduce the chances of endemic diseases reaching epidemic proportions.

(g) **Medical logistic requirements.** Whatever the anticipated level of medical support for civilians, the medical logistic requirements will be greater than those for the force only. Accurate logistic planning will reduce the likelihood of conflict between health services requirements in support of the joint force and those in support of civilians.

(6) All health services units must have the capability to react quickly and decisively to a terrorist incident. Medical treatment facilities should have well-conceived mass casualty control plans and contingency support plans. These plans should consider the urban terrain, population densities, major roads, possible landing zones, location of all medical facilities, and reaction procedures.

e. **Personnel Service Support.** Personnel support has several unique considerations in JUOs. The areas of replacement/rotation policies; morale, welfare, and recreation; contingency operation benefits and entitlements; medical returnees to duty; and casualty reporting take on added importance. Personnel augmentation and manning requirements; joint personnel reception and processing; joint personnel accountability and reporting; military postal services; and NEO may require emphasis.

f. **Legal**

(1) **General.** JUOs are likely to involve myriad unique legal and policy considerations. Because of the nature and complexity of the operational legal issues involved (e.g., law of war, ROE, RUF, detainees, dislocated civilians, negotiations and involvement with local and HN governments), the SJA must be consulted early and frequently.

For further information, see JP 1-04, Legal Support to Military Operations.

(2) **Legal Considerations in JUOs.** The large numbers of civilians potentially affected by a JUO are a major legal concern and increase the requirement for knowledgeable and active legal support to the joint force. Whether these civilians suffer the negative effects of urban combat or benefit from FHA, there are legal requirements and ramifications to every aspect of the operation. Unique aspects of JUOs that raise complex legal issues include, but are not limited to, the proximity or colocation of civilian persons and objects with military objectives, the difficulty of distinguishing combatants from civilians, the potential second- and third-order effects on civilians resulting from attacks on infrastructure, and an adversary's potential use of civilians, protected structures (e.g., hospitals), and sensitive infrastructure as a shield to deter US or multinational attacks.

(3) Law of war imposes the obligation on the commander to evaluate all uses of force in light of certain principles. They are:

(a) **Military Necessity.** That principle which justifies those measures not forbidden by international law which are indispensable for securing the complete submission of the enemy as soon as possible. It authorizes that use of force required to accomplish the mission, but does not authorize acts otherwise prohibited by the law of war.

(b) **Unnecessary Suffering.** The right of combatants to adopt means of injuring the enemy is not unlimited. Military personnel may not use means or methods that are, per se, calculated to cause unnecessary suffering, nor may they use otherwise lawful arms in a manner that causes unnecessary suffering. In determining whether a means or method of warfare causes unnecessary suffering, the commander should consult with their SJA.

(c) **Distinction.** This principle is fundamental to avoiding unnecessary suffering. The principle of distinction requires that military operations be directed at combatants and military targets, not civilians or civilian property. Military force may be directed only against military objects or objectives, and not against civilian objects.

(d) **Proportionality.** This principle requires the commander to weigh whether potential attacks may be expected to cause incidental loss of civilian life, injury to civilians, damage to civilian objects, or a combination thereof, which would be excessive in relation to the concrete and direct military advantage anticipated by those attacks.

(4) One of the major areas affected by the law of war is **targeting.** Military power may be directed against an enemy nation's ability to wage war, and not against its civilian population as such. The law of war authorizes the attack of military objectives, while prohibiting the intentional attack of the enemy civilian population (individual civilians not taking a direct part in hostilities) or civilian objects. A range of counter personnel and counter materiel nonlethal capabilities exist which provide the JFC flexibility in targeting options. Creating nonlethal effects to support achievement of tactical or operational objectives can serve to enhance the legitimacy of the joint force by applying only that force necessary to accomplish the mission.

(5) The law of war and DOD policy prohibit or restrict the use of certain weapons such as landmines, booby traps, incendiary devices, and lasers specifically designed to cause permanent blindness. Some aspects of the law of war provisions are particularly relevant to JUOs and uses of these weapons must be part of the legal review conducted of all operation plans.

(6) **War crimes** are certain violations of the law of war by any person or persons, military or civilian. A key to preventing war crimes by US or multinational forces is awareness of the factors that have historically led to their commission. Several of these factors are frequent products of urban combat:

(a) High friendly losses;

(b) High turnover rate in the chain of command;

(c) Dehumanization of the adversary;

(d) Poorly trained or inexperienced troops;

(e) The lack of a clearly defined adversary;

(f) Unclear orders;

(g) High frustration level among the troops; and

(h) Lack of training on and lack of understanding of the law of war, ROE, and related guidance.

(7) The legal requirements and prohibitions regarding civilians are not found in a single legal source. Laws **protecting civilians** include a wide array of treaties, customary international law, HN laws, agreements, and policy including the Hague Conventions and the four Geneva Conventions, that cover civilian protection. The SJA or legal advisor must examine the purpose and method of the operation to determine how and to what extent civilians might be affected. The SJA or legal advisor can then advise the commander on the legal ramifications of the operation and, more importantly, provide significant support as the specific ROE for the operation are developed.

(8) **ROE** are directives issued by competent military authority that delineate the circumstances and limitations under which US forces will initiate and/or continue combat engagement with other forces encountered. Legal factors are but one element of the ROE; nonlegal issues such as national policy and political objectives also play an essential role in the drafting of ROE. Often the ROE will include some restrictions on weapons and targets, and provide the operational commander with guidelines to ensure the greatest possible protection of civilians consistent with military necessity.

(9) **Other legal considerations** applicable to JUOs fall into the area of administrative law, environmental law, contracts, and fiscal law (acquisitions) and claims. These areas require knowledge of US and HN laws, international law, and USG regulations. These types of legal issues are generally applicable to peacetime exercises and deployments as well as military operations. Special operations have unique legal issues that should be addressed by SJAs familiar not only with the law, but also with the nature and requirements of those operations.

APPENDIX A
JOINT INTELLIGENCE PREPARATION OF THE
OPERATIONAL ENVIRONMENT IN URBAN AREAS

1. General

a. JIPOE is the analytical process used by intelligence organizations to produce intelligence assessments, estimates, and other intelligence products in support of the JFC's decision-making process. It is a continuous process that assists JFCs and their staffs in achieving information superiority by identifying adversary COGs, focusing intelligence collection at the right time and place, and analyzing the impact of the operational environment on military operations.

b. The JIPOE process also emphasizes a holistic approach by analyzing both military and nonmilitary aspects of the operational environment that are relevant to the joint mission. This holistic approach enables JIPOE analysts to develop a general assessment of the adversary's diplomatic, informational, military, and economic options.

c. The JFC evaluates the urban operational environment to determine the implications for military operations. This evaluation extends from complex terrain considerations to the even more complex impact of the sheer number of actors operating in an urban operational environment. There may be adversary military troops, criminal gangs, vigilantes, and paramilitary factions operating among the civilian population. The situation may be further complicated by the presence of nonmilitary government departments and agencies, to include intelligence, law enforcement, and other specialized entities or religious/social influencers and cultural norms/expectations. Crucial to planning operations that will be conducted in an urban environment is the understanding gained by both JIPOE and mission analysis.

d. JIPOE must particularly consider the impact of the civilians, whose normal, though potentially significant, activities and presence in the urban area may be substantial and dynamic. **The availability of highly trained individuals who understand the culture and the language will prove indispensable to commanders at all levels in sorting out combatants and civilians.** Determining the ethnic and religious composition of the population and, if possible, their intent (e.g., to flee or remain in the urban areas, to remain neutral, or support one side of the conflict) may prove crucial. Human behavior is difficult to predict and control on a mass scale; to do so with persons of a different culture under the strains of conflict is a significant requirement of any JUO. For example, combat may drive agricultural workers from the surrounding areas into the perceived shelter of the urban environment, which may leave fields unattended. The consequence may contribute to famine and the spread of diseases, further stress limited service capabilities, create more crime, and exacerbate cultural tensions. These potential consequences highlight the need for more intelligence capabilities in an urban setting, specifically the importance of HUMINT.

e. **JIPOE for a JUO** will likely require inputs, collaboration, and dialogue with numerous agencies, some of which are not only external to DOD but the USG as well.

Joint forces must have the technical capability and the operational acumen to use multisource information and intelligence fusion, rapid analysis, and dissemination down to the lowest level. Before and during hostilities within the theater, ground, airborne, maritime, and space-based ISR assets may bridge the information gap often present in an enclosed and quickly changing environment such as the urban environment.

f. The densities of urban areas present numerous challenges for the intelligence analyst because the same factors that complicate the operational aspects of JUOs—the terrain, infrastructure, and population—also stress the existing methods of collection, intelligence analysis, and decision making. Unique urban attributes generate large quantities of information that challenge existing JIPOE techniques. For JIPOE to remain effective for a JUO, its analysis must include a city's unique attributes—buildings, infrastructure, and people—along with an evaluation of the attributes traditionally included in JIPOE, namely, the underlying terrain and the known threat.

2. Joint Intelligence Preparation of the Operational Environment Process for Joint Operations in an Urban Environment

a. In JUOs, tactical-level detail often has operational or strategic significance. Therefore, JIPOE support to JUOs must provide a finer degree of detail than would be required of operations over a broader operational area. JIPOE products (e.g., modified combined obstacle overlays, doctrinal templates, situation templates, and event templates) should be tailored to the situation, but should follow the general formats prescribed in JP 2-01.3, *Joint Intelligence Preparation of the Operational Environment*. Recognizing what is unknown and adapting guidance to units based on these gaps in information are fundamental to the effectiveness of the ever-ongoing JIPOE process. JIPOE support to JUOs follows the basic four-step process outlined below.

b. **Define the Operational Environment**

(1) The procedures for delineating an urban area of operations (AO) fundamentally differ little from those used for other terrain; however, the elements considered in each may be both more numerous and more complex. Analysis in support of JUOs is often more complicated than when the mission involves a readily identified enemy on open terrain. Specified, implied, and essential tasks may be very heterogeneous and will often include such diverse responsibilities as combat actions directed against the enemy, support activities to ensure that civilians do not needlessly suffer, and stability requirements only marginally related to the maneuver and combat support demands. This may result in a greater number of specified and implied tasks. Picking out the essential tasks from this mass becomes especially difficult. In addition, actions taken by a friendly or opposing unit can lead to several unintended consequences. The 1968 fighting in Hue, for instance, caused large numbers of South Vietnamese civilians to seek refuge with their American allies, placing unanticipated demands on US logistics and tactical units. The Marine Corps has articulated such possibilities in its "three-block war" concept: three adjacent city blocks may simultaneously present a commander with combat, stability, and support taskings. Mission articulation needs to balance these myriad demands with unit capabilities when defining AOs.

(2) Other attributes may be similarly complicated during JUOs. The enemy can include a recognizably uniformed adversary, but threat analysis will also have to review many civilian, police, and paramilitary groups. Some of these will favor the enemy, others friendly forces, while yet others will seek only to be left alone by opposing factions. Even this too simply states the probable state of affairs. Groups are fickle in their favoritism. Their dispositions may repeatedly change in response to propaganda, bribes, coercion, or other pressures. Further, demographic groups are by no means homogeneous in their support; a clan aligned with one side may well have members with agendas diverging from those of their leaders.

(3) Terrain includes not only the natural surface confronted during any military undertaking, but also the aforementioned structures on it, beneath it, and the infrastructure throughout. Building construction type will influence the force needed for a particular mission and the type of equipment required. Yet analysis must delve far deeper than simple identification of a feature's characteristics. The number of such features per unit space (density) and the density of features within features (e.g., rooms within apartments within an apartment building) will similarly have a significant influence on the quantity and composition of a force selected for a given urban mission. In addition, there might exist a single street, avenue, or boulevard that might be assigned as its own AO because of buildings of religious, governmental, or cultural importance, such as LeLoi Street in Hue or Pennsylvania Avenue in Washington, DC.

(4) The forces available for actions in built-up areas cannot be determined using traditional force design; the number of tasks and varied terrain may demand extraordinary force ratios, nontraditional force structures, or other adjustments. The time necessary for a JUO cannot be extrapolated from that needed to maneuver on less-complex terrain. The urban topography increases the overall surface area that the proposed mission will involve; intersections and multiple layers of "ground" increase the number of fronts that drain a unit of men, materiel, and time. Finally, civilians complicate matters not only from the perspective of threat as noted above, but also from that of the support they require to survive, the constraints their presence imposes on friendly force firepower employment, and the need to coordinate with agencies seeking to assist those in need. The density of the population will impact on the TTP most appropriate for a mission, as it will on the demand for food, water, medical care, and the likelihood of epidemics. Whereas rural environments generally contain fairly homogeneous social groups, the requirements for cultural awareness in towns and cities are complicated by the multiplicity of indigenous and international demographic factions. In short, buildings, infrastructure, and diverse populations tend to introduce intricacies into every element of the process of defining the AO.

(5) Compared to other types of operations, civilian considerations have a disproportionately large influence on JUOs. Social and cultural awareness is essential to helping see and understand the city as its residents understand it. An educated perspective assists in identifying key features of the population and terrain. What are the defining social characteristics? Do the apparent instruments of control (police, politicians) represent the people or some other interest group? How are the neighborhoods configured? Are they segregated by physical or ethnic boundaries? What are the true sources of power and

influence in the area of concern? Answers to these kinds of questions will lead to better understanding of the urban environment.

(6) Figure A-1 provides several sample questions that might be asked during the AO and AOI definition processes. The MCIA 2700-002-03, *Urban Generic Information Requirements Handbook (UGIRH)*, includes other questions of potential value during analysis for the first step of the JIPOE process.

(7) The vertical character of the AO, indeterminable via most overhead imagery, could dramatically influence helicopter and tiltrotor aircraft operations. Pending determination of whether rotary-wing support is feasible, an assigned AO may have to be drawn to include additional ground-level LOCs.

(8) **Urban AOIs.** Urban AOIs are geographic areas from which information and intelligence are required to plan and execute successful operations. Traditional JIPOE usually limits the AOI to geographical areas from which the threat has the ability to jeopardize friendly force mission accomplishment. Urban AOIs must encompass more than this. Urban architecture, social and physical infrastructure, and populations are entities linked by physical, economic, political, social, and cultural ties. The delineation of urban AOIs must consider how these many links can influence mission accomplishment within the AO.

(a) Building design and physical infrastructure may influence AOI definition. Street layout, LOS into and out of the AO, and subterranean access are three possible considerations of importance. Designation of nodal AOIs (those noncontiguous to the AO)

Illustrative Questions for Defining the Area of Operations and Area of Interest

- What types of buildings are in the proposed area of operations (AO)?
- What is the interrelationship between the infrastructure in the proposed AO and that in other operational areas?
- Are there clear demographic boundaries that have a greater influence on mission success than do readily identifiable physical boundaries?
- How can the AO be defined to ease coordination between the unit and representatives of key demographic or governmental groups?
- How are demographic groups structured within the AO?
- Are there unique or culturally salient buildings within the area of concern?
- Are there particular buildings or areas that are currently contested among different demographic groups?
- Are there significant streets, avenues, or boulevards that contain key buildings of government, religious, or cultural interest?

Figure A-1. Illustrative Questions for Defining the Area of Operations and Area of Interest

---

may also be warranted. Monitoring local fire stations, police headquarters, religious centers, and the like could provide information on civil readiness and pending crises. Information on such areas could also explain what might mistakenly appear to be activities of potential concern, such as sudden movements of large numbers of the indigenous population due to a pending sports event.

(b) Urban infrastructure more clearly demonstrates the need to consider geographically distant or disconnected components of the AOI. Electrical wires, water treatment and supply systems, and media outlets are among the elements to consider. Is the electricity used within the AO generated in a distant area? Are there other means of energy transmission? Is electricity necessary for mission accomplishment? Are there antennas or transmission elements outside of the AO that can influence those within it?

(c) Population groups complicate the AOI definition not only because of their widespread interrelationships, but also because of their mobility. Citizens residing in the AO may move to another area for reasons as straightforward as commuting to work or for less savory purposes that have significant mission implications. NGOs may deliberately or inadvertently influence civilian actions in ways that could likewise concern a military force. These organizations' activities are the result of decisions made both locally and at headquarters that may be thousands of miles distant. There may be a need to monitor these decisions if they could impact friendly force operations. Insurgent groups, organized crime elements, and other potential threats may receive support from diaspora or other entities in networks that channel funds, weapons, or other resources to groups within the AO. Recognizing and monitoring such relationships could be critical to both local operations and those distant from the AO.

(d) The presence of media is also important to consider when delineating the AOI. Television, radio signals, the Internet, and other forms of media can all connect the AO with nonadjacent outside areas. The media can affect the PA and IO component of any mission as critically as the physical component. Being able to identify means of transmission and possible audiences to any kind of mission becomes a key component of defining an AOI for an operation in an urban environment.

(9) Obviously the scope of influences pertinent to a unit's mission can potentially overwhelm its limited information-collection and processing capabilities. Barring the addition of supplemental assets, commanders and their staffs will have to focus on issues of notable importance while relegating the others to a lower priority. Ultimately the discrimination will depend on two questions. Answering these questions will assist in identifying second- and higher-order effects of decisions and actions, a key element in properly defining the AOI:

(a) Could the issue under consideration influence actions in the AO so as to demonstrably affect mission accomplishment?

(b) If so, how?

c. **Describe the impact of the operational environment.** The urban operational environment contains significant differences from other environments. These differences include more complex physical terrain, concentrated infrastructure, and relatively dense population. JIPOE analysts help develop a holistic view of the operational environment by analyzing the physical and nonphysical aspects of the operational environment, and by developing a systems perspective of relevant PMESII links and nodes. This step begins with the identification and analysis of all militarily significant existing and projected characteristics of the operational environment. These characteristics are then analyzed to determine their impact on the capabilities and broad COAs of both adversary and friendly forces. Products developed during this step might include, but are not limited to, overlays and matrices that depict the military impact of geography, meteorological factors, demographics, and the information environment. Other products may include network analysis diagrams associated with adversary and neutral PMESII and other systems.

(1) Because of a population's ability to affect a military operation in a variety of ways, analysis should place a primary focus on the city's inhabitants. With a better understanding of the people who drive urban activity, analysis of other urban features such as building and infrastructure can be better focused to address the unit's mission and the needs of the people.

(2) **Population Analysis.** Accommodating the social fabric of a city is potentially the most influential factor in the conduct of a JUO. The fastest way to damage the legitimacy of an operation is to ignore or violate social mores or precepts of a particular population. Any discussion of a city's population requires a two-pronged approach. Developing a clear picture of a city's population requires delineating its primary attributes, such as age, wealth, gender, ethnicity, religion, and employment statistics. Collecting this information and reporting its significance is considered demographic analysis. The second component, cultural intelligence, describes the process by which cultural information— issues/grievances, mores, values, relationships and rivalries between particular groups, to name a few—is incorporated with demographic information to uncover the underlying characteristics of the population that the unit will face. Demographic analysis describes the physical characteristics of a population group, while cultural intelligence helps explain the behavior and moral characteristics of a population group.

(3) **Demographic Analysis and Cultural Intelligence.** Demographic analysis seeks to characterize population groups and subgroups within a commander's operational area. Both the MCIA 2700-002-03, *Urban Generic Information Requirements Handbook (UGIRH),* and Army FM 2-91.4, *Intelligence Support to Urban Operations,* provide useful checklists of the factors that should be considered when conducting demographic analysis. Using these lists, the analyst can create pictures—often in the form of templates, overlays, or descriptions—of a city's key societal characteristics. They delineate the critical factors that define each population group and show where differences exist. Some examples are population status overlay, congregation points overlay, building type overlay, traffic conditions, times and locations, nocturnal and diurnal conditions, and overlay of most likely threat locations.

(a) These tools only generate a picture of a city based on static information. They do not necessarily describe the population as a thinking component of the operational area, nor do they attribute any type of dynamism or reactiveness to the people. Often, the joint operation planning process might require a more in-depth understanding of the population. How demographic traits influence the population's actions, expectations, and relationships with other groups within the AO, associated AOI, and operational environment might be critical to maintaining stability within the host city. This information might also prove useful in establishing legitimacy or obtaining allegiance from populations. It will be critical for some IO efforts; without cultural understanding, a MISO mission, for example, might be completely ineffective.

(b) Understanding a culture means more than knowing the habits and likes and dislikes of a neighborhood's inhabitants; it means making a concerted effort to explain the underlying value system which informs these actions, and thus provide the JFC with a greater awareness of how the local populace will affect and be affected by operations. It augments demographic analysis by describing how demographic traits and relationships between groups can act, or have already acted, to stabilize or destabilize conditions. Some examples of cultural intelligence tools include lists and timelines of salient cultural and political events, culture description or cultural comparison charts or matrices, a line of confrontation overlay or matrix, a culturally significant structures overlay, "power" templates, and a status quo ante bellum overlay.

(4) There are two additional cultural intelligence products that seek to assist in developing a deeper understanding of how the population within the operational area can actively affect the ongoing operation. Both are dynamic tools—they should be constantly updated to measure changing conditions. These products are also introduced in very simplified form, for use in any type of operation. They can be modified, refined, augmented, and automated to suit the more sophisticated needs of intelligence or law enforcement agencies.

(a) **Relationship Matrices.** Relationship matrices are intended to depict the nature of relationships between elements of the operational area. The elements can include members from the civilian population, the friendly force, IGOs, and an adversarial group. Utility infrastructure, significant buildings, and media might also be included. The nature of the relationship between two or more components includes measures of contention, collusion, or dependency. The purpose of this product is to demonstrate graphically how each component of the city interacts with the others and whether these interactions promote or degrade the likelihood of mission success. The relationships represented in the matrix can also begin to help the analysts in deciphering how to best use the relationship to help shape the environment.

For an example of a relationship matrix, see FM 2-91.4, Intelligence Support to Urban Operations.

(b) **Perception Assessment Matrices.** Perception is the interpretation of sensory input from seeing, hearing, smelling, tasting, or touching. Perception is also influenced by physiological capacities, frames of reference, learning, past experiences, and cultural and social environments. Friendly force activities intended to be benign or benevolent might have negative results if a population's perceptions are not first investigated and subsequently measured or managed. This is true because perceptions—more than reality—drive decision making, and in turn, could influence the reactions of entire populations. The perception assessment matrix seeks to provide some measure of effectiveness (MOE) for the unit's ability to maintain legitimacy during an operation. In this sense, the matrix can also be used to directly measure the effectiveness of the unit's CA, PA, and MISO efforts.

For an example of a perception assessment matrix, see FM 2-91.4, Intelligence Support to Urban Operations.

   <u>1.</u> Perception can work counter to operational objectives. Perceptions should therefore be assessed both before and throughout an operation. Although it is not possible to read the minds of the population, there are several means to measure its perceptions.

   <u>a.</u> Demographic analysis and cultural intelligence are key components of perception analysis.

   <u>b.</u> Understanding a population's history can help predict expectations and reactions.

   <u>c.</u> HUMINT can provide information on population perceptions.

   <u>d.</u> Reactions and key activities can be carefully observed in order to decipher whether people act based on real conditions or perceived conditions.

   <u>e.</u> Editorial and opinion pieces of relevant newspapers can be monitored for changes in tone or opinion shifts that can steer or may be reacting to the opinions of a population group.

   <u>2.</u> Perception assessment matrices aim to measure the disparities between friendly force actions and what population groups perceive. In addition to trying to assess the perceptions of each population group within an operational area, it might serve the interests of the unit to assess its own perceptions of its activities. Are members of the unit exhibiting decidedly Western or American values that are not appreciated by the HN population? Are embedded American beliefs preventing the unit from understanding the HN population or its multinational partners? Is what the intelligence and command staff is perceiving really what is going on in the operational area? Does the population believe what the unit believes? Is there something that is part of the population's (or a subgroup's) perception that can be detrimental to the unit? All these questions can begin to be addressed by the unit's scrutinizing its view of an operation.

   (5) **Multinational, NGO, and IGO Analysis.** Given the scope of US alliances, the likelihood that US forces will work side by side with forces of other nations during any type of operation is virtually guaranteed. Humanitarian obligations also necessitate the presence of NGOs and IGOs to assist the local populace. During domestic operations,

soldiers will work alongside local police officers, firefighters, National Guard troops, and other actors not inherent to their unit.

(a) Civilian actors can be beneficial sources of HN cultural information. During the 1999 fighting in Kosovo, the Red Cross provided the most accurate figures on the number of Kosovo refugees, helping US and other coalition services to estimate the appropriate level of support required to handle their needs. Civilian agencies also develop a network of influential contacts, compile historical and specialty archives, and establish relationships with local leaders and business people. They understand the infrastructure of the region, and the political and economic influences. International aid organizations sometimes keep up-to-date web sites with maps and pertinent information on local and regional areas that could be of potential value to military planners.

(b) Partners in a multinational environment have different capabilities, procedures, doctrine, ROE, and methods of disclosing information. These differences can be at once frustrating and useful. For instance, soldiers of the United Kingdom and US working side by side in Bosnia had different methods of collecting and sharing intelligence. This frustrated intelligence analysts' ability to work as a cohesive group but provided HUMINT resources to the US that would not otherwise have been available.

(c) Multinational, NGO, and IGO analysis should seek to list all the key similarities and differences among all groups in an operational area. Population status overlays or relationship matrices that contain categories like ROE, information-sharing capabilities, aid resources, and other pieces of relevant information can be constructed to evaluate each of the nonorganic actors with which the joint force is dealing. A relationship matrix focusing on how the US relates to each nonorganic actor and ways in which those actors might pursue relationships with members of the population will also be helpful in determining how multinational force members, NGOs, the media, and other participants could influence the mission. A matrix containing each NGO's capabilities, location, and relationships will assist both operators and intelligence analysts.

(6) **Urban Weather Analysis.** Along with typical weather patterns, cities have their own microclimates that can affect operations. Dust, smog, wind channeling, night illumination, and sun reflection off buildings are all conditions that could alter a unit's normal TTP. These conditions are often transitory or initiated by friendly force actions. Dust plumes from helicopters are one example. There are certain conditions related to natural occurrences that, although not necessarily weather-related, fit most logically into the weather analysis category. For instance, certain cities, or parts of a city, may have a particular odor that can distract the soldier. A product used to map the path this odor generally follows might better prepare the soldier for the potential distraction. This same logic can be used to track how hazardous gases can disperse in the atmosphere, or how a fire might spread. Therefore, in addition to the weather products that are traditionally created for all types of operations, some that are specifically adapted to accommodate urban weather effects must also be constructed. Considerations that might be included in urban weather analysis are:

(a) Dust clouds created by helicopter or tiltrotor aircraft blades kicking up the dirt from the street, inhibiting troop movement and deployment.

(b) Extreme heat from being confined to small places or from the sun reflecting off asphalt may also hamper troop effectiveness.

(c) The city's effect on night operations may also be significant. The extra luminescence provided by the ambient light of the city may neutralize the perceived advantage of US night vision technology. In addition, residents of the city are familiar with its layout and can maneuver easily in darkness.

(d) Smog inversion layers are common over cities. An inversion layer may trap dust, smoke, and chemicals in the air that can be detrimental to the health of soldiers. If the conditions are severe enough, protective gas masks may be needed during some types of operations. Weather analysis products for urban JIPOE are similar to those for traditional JIPOE but should include these peculiarities.

(7) **Terrain and Infrastructure.** The analysis must consider the following factors:

(a) **Urban terrain:** building construction, subterranean features, and physical layout and subdivisions of the urban area.

(b) **Infrastructure**

1. Key facilities, (e.g., CBRN-related: pharmaceutical, chemical, nuclear).

2. Critical urban services (e.g., schools, municipal buildings).

3. Power plants (e.g., nuclear, conventional, hydroelectric).

4. Water system (e.g., dams, reservoirs, aqueducts, pumping stations).

5. Sewage and waste disposal.

6. Medical facilities.

7. Communications lines and nodes.

8. Ports and harbors.

9. Airfields.

10. Helicopter landing zones.

11. Roadways.

12. Railways and rail yards.

13. Bridges.

14. Subways.

15. Civil defense shelters.

16. Petroleum and natural gas lines and storage facilities.

17. Resources and material production.

(c) Surrounding environs: sources of electric power generation (e.g., lakes, rivers), sources of food and water, and base camps or support areas for insurgents.

(d) Adjoining countries' terrain and airspace restrictions.

d. **Evaluate the Adversary and Other Relevant Actors.** In JUOs, the adversary and other relevant actors could be greatly different from an adversary and other relevant actors normally associated with operations in nonurban environments. The third step in the JIPOE process identifies and evaluates the adversary's military and relevant objectives, their critical factors, limitations, and the doctrine, TTP employed by adversary forces, absent any constraints that may be imposed by the operational environment. During this step, models are developed that accurately portray how adversary forces normally execute military operations or how they have reacted to specific military situations in the past. Adversaries may choose to make widespread use of snipers, ambushes, and HUMINT networks, and may choose to deliberately avoid decisive engagements.

(1) **The Challenge of Threat Evaluation for JUOs.** The people, buildings, and infrastructure in an urban area inhibit straightforward threat evaluation by obscuring both threat identity and threat capabilities, and by introducing myriad other influences that may negatively, positively, or benignly influence friendly force operations. There is also a multitude of such possible threats and influences. A variety of active, passive, and latent population elements can potentially influence friendly and enemy (if present) force operations in any type of urban mission. Being able to assess the level of threat or opportunity each element imposes is fundamental to mission success.

(2) The greater density and multiple interrelationships of individuals found in built-up areas increase the complexity of categorization. Nevertheless, for the purposes of planning, force protection, and conducting operations it is necessary to have a way to place each group on a continuum that effectively depicts "threatening" and "nonthreatening" sectors of the population.

(3) The effort is not a one-time undertaking. The categorization will require constant review. Groups and individuals can be cajoled, forced, or co-opted into providing or withholding services to either the friendly or opposing force. The posture of groups, and members within groups, should therefore be considered variable.

(4) Even seemingly passive and law-abiding members of a populace may conduct themselves in unexpected ways given the right conditions. During the Los Angeles riots of 1992, for example, looting and destruction of property was perpetrated by otherwise law-abiding citizens. The opportunistic nature of conditions is one cause of this phenomenon.

Instability, the breakdown of legal authority, and the chance to immerse oneself in the protective environment of a crowd are all conditions that stimulate such behavior. All are conditions frequently apparent during operations in urban areas.

(5) Population groups or individuals can unwittingly interfere with operations and thereby increase friendly force exposure. Refugee flows and members of the media have already been used as examples of how people can impede friendly force actions by merely doing what is necessary for their own well-being.

(6) Groups or individuals can also be manipulated by either the friendly or opposing force, by other parties, or by events themselves. Such manipulation may be with or without the knowledge of the subjects influenced. A captured opponent asked to provide HUMINT is an example of the former circumstance; the use of MISO or CAO to influence the activity of a population exemplifies the latter.

(7) These and other challenges require modification of JIPOE traditional step three. Step three for a JUO must first identify the elements, human and otherwise, that can harm, interfere with, or otherwise significantly influence friendly force activities. Once identified, the most mission-significant elements can be prioritized for fuller evaluation. Others can be handled as time allows. Step three should include the following:

(a) An identification phase in which all population groups and subgroups are arrayed along a continuum denoting their interests relative to the friendly force (or to each other). Entities that can threaten, interfere with, or otherwise significantly influence operations are noted for further evaluation.

(b) A prioritization of these entities based on the degree to which they can impact mission accomplishment.

(c) Evaluation that includes TTP perhaps not generally encountered in other environments.

(8) **Urban Adversary and Relevant Influences Evaluation.** Strategies and tactics can take a variety of forms; from no-tech and low-tech approaches to high-tech. These adversaries may have no known doctrine. What can be known about them is what can be gained from the lessons-learned literature and recent journalistic accounts of urban battles, some of which is listed below. This information is meant to be illustrative, not comprehensive. It can be used as a starting point in identifying the ways that an adversary might fight in an urban environment. Clearly, the modern urban adversary does not rely entirely on maneuver warfare to win battles—his technological inferiority and the nature of the terrain do not allow it. This fact makes it very difficult to identify high-value targets associated with adversary tactics. There may be no key C2 node to target. Frequently there is no flank against which to advance. The intelligence analyst needs to determine ways to neutralize tactics such as those described below; related high-value targets and COGs may be as nontraditional as are the tactics themselves.

**EXAMPLES OF ENEMY URBAN WARFARE
TACTICS, STRATEGIES, AND WEAPONS**

Units tend to be small, somewhat autonomous groups that require limited guidance and intergroup communication.

Decentralization of Chechen command and control created difficulties for the Russians during both battles for Grozny. Chechen groups employed varied and nontraditional tactics, at times deliberately, in other instances because small-unit leaders were adapting to situations they had failed to foresee.

Weapon systems tend to be small and portable.

A typical urban threat arsenal might contain rifles, rocket-propelled grenades (RPGs), and other antitank weapons. Employing such weapons requires little preliminary training or logistical support, but they can be extremely effective. Urban canyons and close quarters make these hand-held weapons all the more effective. Chechen hunter-killer RPG teams were fundamental to neutralizing the Russian armor threat in Grozny.

Commercial off-the-shelf (COTS) technologies are common.

Scanners, mobile TV equipment, jammers, radios, and computers help a less sophisticated force in its efforts to close the technological gap between itself and a regular military organization. Adversaries confronted in Mogadishu, Chechnya, Northern Ireland, Bosnia, and Kosovo all made use of COTS technologies.

Tactics include kidnappings, swarming, raids, ambushes, and the use of snipers, assassinations, and booby traps.

The Provisional Irish Republican Army, Chechens, and Colombian guerillas are all known to have used these tactics. An important element in their employment is the psychological effect they have on the adversary. That an attack can come from any one of five directions—above, below, from the side, front, or behind—increases the degree of mental stress.

Urban adversaries battle for hearts and minds through the use of information, disinformation, propaganda, and manipulation of the press.

Information operations are increasingly critical to the urban adversary. Because he is striking at the US will to fight, one of the asymmetric adversary's primary methods is to use information warfare tactics. They are relatively cheap and nonlethal. It is generally accepted that Russia lost the information warfare battle during the first Grozny invasion. Media were allowed almost unlimited access to the fighting. As a result, Russian public support for the fighting was low. During the second campaign, media personnel were restricted from entering the operational area and were given stories approved by Russian military or government officials. Domestic support for the Russians was markedly improved as a result.

Thwarting the high-technology assets of a Western force is sought via low-tech or no-tech means.

During the North Atlantic Treaty Organization (NATO) air strikes on Kosovo, the Serbs used obscurants and other methods to disrupt precision-guided munitions engagements. In Mogadishu, unarmed civilians employed kites in attempts to down American helicopters.

The restrictions placed on friendly force activities by treaties, laws of land warfare, and rules of engagement are frequently exploited.

The Chechens positioned a command post in a hospital, demonstrating their disregard for international law. Dropping live power lines over roadways or poisoning water supplies to create panic are other examples of how terror can be used by those who consider themselves unencumbered by Geneva Convention and other standards.

Military information support operations (MISO) [formerly psychological operations (PSYOP)], deception, civil affairs, and public affairs are often employed.

The two battles for Grozny offer considerable anecdotal evidence of MISO [PSYOP] and deception use. The Chechens altered Russian operations by giving commands in Russian on their enemy's radio nets. Chechens fired from behind the hanging bodies (alive or dead) of Russian soldiers and booby trapped Russian wounded. Carlos Marighella, in his treatise the *Mini-Manual for the Urban Guerilla,* instructs his readers to undermine the psyche of the more advanced enemy.

Adversaries use the three-dimensional character of urban terrain to their advantage—operating from all four sides, above, and below.

The Chechens often secured the top floors of buildings in Grozny. Once Russian soldiers entered the building, the Chechens would begin firing through the floor.

Adversaries use the interconnectedness of the city to exploit nodal capabilities.

Yugoslav President Slobodan Milosevic demonstrated the power of this capability. "By ingenuity, discreet purchases and some help from its neighbors, Milosevic's government has kept electricity flowing despite NATO's high-tech strikes against distribution grids." In addition, "transnational communities, or diasporas, are taking on new importance. Diasporas provide money, arms, fighters, and leaders to their ancestral groups struggling for freedom."

SOURCE: *Street Smart Intelligence:*
Preparation of the Battlefield
for Urban Operations

e. **Determine Adversary and Other Relevant Actors COAs.** COA development for JIPOE in an urban environment, the fourth step, follows the same procedures as traditional JIPOE. Rather than just consider the enemy, however, COA development considerations must be made for each relevant population group. The final step of urban JIPOE should seek to develop a COA for groups that are potential threats, as well as a COA for groups that might act together against the joint force. COA should also be developed for groups that do not at the outset appear to be threatening but might, because of a series of events, become involved in activities that could impact the overall mission of the unit. The following factors should be considered when determining possible adversary COAs in urban environments.

(1) Identify each population group's desired end state. The interests and intentions of each of the population elements, identified in step three of urban JIPOE, can help to define the desired end state for each of the identified relevant populations. This information is derived from cultural intelligence, HUMINT, media analysis, and other sources.

(2) Work backward, from end state to initiation point, to develop COAs for each non-US actor. For this step, deriving the capabilities and intentions of each relevant population group will assist in developing COAs and identifying their associated named AOIs and target AOIs. The capabilities matrix in conjunction with the relationship matrix can be used to help build a COA for each relevant group. An additional technique involves analysis of COAs that seem unlikely. Start with an assumption that an unexpected event has actually occurred. Then, work backward to explain how this could have happened. This will help develop a list of COAs that may not otherwise have been considered. These techniques can generate a COA for each population group. In addition, when evaluating a known adversary for a combat operation, they can be used in conjunction with any analysis of known and supposed tactics of the adversarial force to create enemy COAs. The following sample questions can assist when developing these COAs.

(a) Does the population element in question have all of the capabilities required to complete the COA?

(b) Does the population element have the capability to make the US or other population elements resident in the AO believe that it can complete the proposed COA?

(c) Does the population element know of its inherent capability, or is the capability something that can unwittingly affect operations?

(d) How is each of the capabilities going to be integrated in order to attain the desired end state?

(e) Are there several different ways to integrate capabilities to attain the desired end state?

(f) What are the interests of the relevant groups? Can they be shaped by the friendly or adversarial force? Have they been shaped already?

(g) What are the friendly force critical vulnerabilities? Which population groups are aware of these critical vulnerabilities?

UNINTENDED CONSEQUENCES

An example of several immediate and lasting higher-order effects can be gleaned from the NATO [North Atlantic Treaty Organization] bombing of Kosovo in 2000. Almost immediately, Kosovo suffered a refugee problem when Serbs reacted by purging entire areas of Albanian residents. This migration had the second-order effect of complicating NATO targeting, for the Serbs used the refugees as cover by positioning them close to their own forces, deliberately putting them at risk should NATO aircraft engage the legitimate targets. Further, at the operational and strategic levels, the massive population displacement created shelter and sustenance shortfalls in Albania, requiring delays in the delivery of military supplies so that tents, food, and other aid could be provided to refugee camps.

SOURCE: *Street Smart Intelligence:*
Preparation of the Battlefield
for Urban Operations

(h) What are the known tactics of the adversary?

(3) **Analyzing the Higher-Order Effects.** COA development too rarely considers how activities—friendly force, enemy, or civilian—might produce unintended consequences. The likelihood of such second- and higher-order effects are of notable concern in urban environments. The increased density of individuals, infrastructure, and buildings means that a given action is more likely to have unintended consequences; further, those consequences will be more widely felt and their impact will spread in less time than in other environments. For instance, a broken sewer pipe or chemical spill in the middle of town can immediately disrupt traffic flow over several square kilometers and threaten an outbreak of disease or other problems rapidly spread by citizens or contaminated materials moving about the city. Spillage of the waste can poison the water supply, relied upon by thousands or tens of thousands within a few kilometers of the spill. A military force manned with engineer, transport, and medical personnel sufficient only to care for its own soldiers could find itself quickly overwhelmed by the need to repair the break, coordinate delivery of fresh water, and treat those who might have been affected.

(a) Determining the higher-order effects of an activity is not unlike assessing the reactions of population groups. It involves an evaluation of the interconnectedness of relevant factors and how interactions can cause unintended outcomes. The capabilities matrix introduced in the previous paragraph can assist in determining the relationships that exist in the operational area. There are also several technologies that can help predict the spread of disease or airborne agents that are currently being used by disaster relief agencies and intelligence organizations. These technologies, while useful, do not take into consideration all of the possible consequences that can be imagined.

(b) In short, COA development for step four of urban JIPOE will normally involve far more than evaluation of a single adversary. COAs for all population elements

---

should be considered, prioritized, and incorporated into the process to adequately assess all effects on any type of operation. They must thereafter be continuously monitored and updated to reflect changes in the environment, group dynamics, or interrelationships. JIPOE step four for a JUO expands the scope of traditional JIPOE to assimilate all relationships and interconnections that exist in an urban operational area.

Intentionally Blank

APPENDIX B
ASSESSMENT

1. General

Assessment is a continuous process that measures the overall effectiveness of employing joint force capabilities during military operations and determines the progress toward accomplishing a task, creating a condition, or achieving an objective. A constant challenge in JUOs is the difficulty to effectively analyze progress using systematic reliable indicators and data collection methods. Every JUO will be unique and a standardized assessment cannot be provided in this appendix. This generic discussion of assessment must be tailored to the situation. Success can be measured by a wide variety of measures such as the reduction of ethnic-on-ethnic violence, reduction in crime, reduced IED attacks, or improvement in public utility performance. An assessment criteria used one week may not be valid the subsequent week. Assessment in JUOs can be highly subjective due to variations in urban patterns. Commanders' intuition at all levels may be a useful measure.

For further information on assessment, refer to JP 3-0, Joint Operations, *JP 5-0,* Joint Operation Planning, *and JP 3-60,* Joint Targeting.

2. Measures of Performance

Tactical-level assessment typically uses measures of performance (MOPs) to evaluate task accomplishment. The results of tactical tasks are often physical in nature, but also can reflect the impact on specific functions and systems. Tactical-level assessment may include assessing progress by phase lines; neutralization of enemy forces; control of key terrain or resources; and security, relief, or reconstruction tasks. Assessment of results at the tactical level helps commanders determine operational and strategic progress, so JFCs must have a comprehensive, integrated assessment plan that links assessment activities and measures at all levels.

3. Measures of Effectiveness

MOEs assess changes in system behavior, capability, or operational environment. They measure the attainment of an end state, achievement of an objective, or creation of an effect; they do not measure task performance. These measures typically are more subjective than MOPs, and can be crafted as either qualitative or quantitative. MOEs can be based on quantitative measures to reflect a trend and show progress toward a measurable threshold. In JUOs, measurable results to a particular action may not appear for some time. This time lag complicates assessment enormously, because in the meantime the joint force may have executed other actions, which will make assessing cause and effect even more difficult.

4. Intelligence Assessment in an Urban Environment

An intelligence assessment in the urban environment should include all information relating to the operation within the construct of a framework such as the ASCOPE [areas, structures, capabilities, organizations, people, and events] factors plus weather effects. Illustrative intelligence assessment measures are presented in Figure B-1.

5. Combat Assessment

Combat assessment measures many tactical-level actions and their implications at the operational level as well. Combat assessment typically focuses on determining the results of weapons engagement (with both lethal and nonlethal capabilities), and thus is an important component of joint fires and the joint targeting process. To conduct combat assessment, it is important to fully understand the linkages between the targets and the JFC's objectives, guidance, and desired effects. Combat assessment is composed of three related elements: BDA, MEA, and reattack recommendations or future targeting.

a. **BDA.** The purpose of BDA is to compare post-execution results with the projected results generated during target development. Comprehensive BDA requires a coordinated and integrated effort between joint force intelligence and operations functions. Traditionally, BDA is composed of physical damage assessment, functional damage assessment, and target system assessment, typically taking a three-phased approach to proceed from a micro-level examination of the damage or effects inflicted on a specific target, to ultimately arriving at macro-level conclusions regarding the functional outcomes created in the target system.

b. **MEA.** MEA studies how combat systems performed and the method in which they were applied. It examines the evidence after attacks to determine whether weapons and weapon systems performed as expected. The purpose of MEA is to compare the actual effectiveness of the means employed to their anticipated effectiveness calculated during the capability analysis phase of the joint targeting cycle. The results of MEA support both near-term improvement in force employment tactics and techniques and long-term improvements in lethal and nonlethal capabilities.

c. **Future Targeting or Reattack Recommendations.** Future target nominations and reattack recommendations merge the picture of what was done (BDA) with how it was done (MEA) and compares the result with predetermined MOEs that were developed at the start of the joint targeting cycle. The purposes of this phase in the process are to determine degree of success in achieving objectives and to formulate any required follow-up actions, or to indicate readiness to move on to new tasks in the path to achieving the overall JFC objectives.

6. Assessment Metrics

The staff develops metrics to determine if operations are properly linked to the JFC's overall strategy and the larger hierarchy of operational and national objectives. These metrics evaluate the results achieved during joint operations. Metrics can either be objective (using sensors or personnel to directly observe damage inflicted) or subjective (using indirect means to ascertain results), depending on the metric applied to either the objective or task. Both qualitative and quantitative metrics should be used to avoid unsound or distorted results. Metrics can either be inductive (directly observing the operational environment and building situational awareness cumulatively) or deductive

Illustrative Urban Assessment Measures

Urban Environment Factors	Urban Environment Conditions		
	Red	Amber	Green
Sewage	Sewage/disposal services are unavailable.	Periodic sewage/disposal services.	Constant sewage/ disposal services.
Water	Insufficient amounts of water causing dehydration for the population.	Sufficient amounts of water to prevent population dehydration, but not enough for adequate hygienic support or food production.	Adequate amounts of water for continued health improvements and sustenance programs.
Electricity	Internal electricity is not available.	Operational electricity is able to power essential functions (emergency service, transportation, etc.).	Electricity is readily available to all citizens.
Academics	Schools or teachers unavailable.	Schools are available, but teachers are part time.	Each school has a full-time teacher.
Trash	Trash disposal service unavailable.	Periodic trash disposal service available.	Normal (steady state) trash disposal service available.
Food	Inadequate food supply (growing, harvesting, or importing) for the population. The population cannot sustain itself without assistance. Famine/starvation is imminent for a portion of the population.	Adequate food supplies that prevent immediate famine for the population, but may not sustain a 6-month continuous period without an increase in certain staples.	Food supplies are adequate for the season (normally based on a 1-year continuous period).
Nongovernmental Organizations	Nongovernmental organizations (NGOs) are unavailable.	NGOs are periodically available.	NGOs are on station.
Government	Lawlessness is prevalent. Legislative body, judicial council, or police force are unrecognized.	Local leadership established; functioning legislative body; and police force is recognized.	Appointed officials, legislative/ judicial body instituted, and police force enforces the laws.
Police	No police or corrupt police presence in city.	Some police presence in city.	Constant police presence throughout city.
Media	Community has no regular access to media of any kind (television, Internet, newspaper, or magazine).	Community has limited access to some media.	Community has access to a wide variety of media, including local sources.
Insurgency	A high frequency of violent acts directed against local or governmental agencies with weapons.	A lower frequency of violent acts against local or governmental agencies without weapons.	No indicators of insurgency present.
Ethnic Tension	High activity of protests and frequent incidents that become riotous.	Medium activity that occasionally has serious incidents, but not riotous.	Low activity with infrequent incidents; generally characterized as peaceful gatherings.
Crime	High activity of burglary, robbery, or mugging with the use of a weapon.	Medium activity of petty theft, stealing, and aggravated assault without the use of a weapon.	Low to no activity of abuse; generally characterized by disagreements or civil disputes.
Subversions/ Espionage	Constant subversive articles, sermons, acts, or demonstrations toward local government or elected leadership.	Regular subversive articles, sermons, acts, or demonstrations against the interim government.	No identified subversion directed against the interim government or the multinational forces.

Figure B-1. Illustrative Urban Assessment Measures

(extrapolated from what was previously known of the adversary and operational environment). Success is measured by indications that the effects created are influencing enemy, friendly, and/or neutral activity in desired ways among various target systems.

Intentionally Blank

APPENDIX C
PLANNING CONSIDERATIONS FOR PORT
AND AIRFIELD COMPLEXES

1. General

a. Ports and airfields play a vital role to an expeditionary force. They are generally located in, or very near, urban areas. In many countries, ports and airfields provide the only means through which large numbers of personnel, equipment, and supplies can enter the operational area.

b. In general, most coastal cities were established around seaports, which contributed to the very existence of port cities. Although some port cities have constructed new port facilities which can be found quite some distance from the urban area, the average port is still located in the center of the most heavily populated and congested part of the urban area. Airfields are generally located farther from the built-up sections of the urban area, depending on their size and when they were first established. Older airfields are normally located closer to the heart of the city, while newer airfields can be located miles away from the outskirts of the urban area.

c. Sea and aerial ports should be viewed as a complex. In addition to the terminal itself, the complex may include areas and functions such as driver holding areas, container holding and handling areas, staging and marshaling areas, frustrated cargo holding areas, assembly areas, and land explosive storage and handling areas. Activities might be conducted simultaneously in all of these areas, and all require valuable space on or near the port complex.

2. Planning Considerations

a. The JFC must plan for both the entry into and the sustainment of the joint force in the operational area. Most of the time, this means planning for the use of available ports and airfields.

b. Although planning for the use of ports has somewhat different considerations than planning for airfields, certain general planning considerations pertain to both.

c. In urban combat operations, it may be necessary to target a port or airfield to prevent its use by the adversary. In this case, the same considerations apply as for other key infrastructure, and if future use by the joint force is contemplated, steps should be taken to limit damage. The same is true if land forces need to physically seize the facilities.

d. **Global Distribution Networks.** The four networks of the integrated global distribution system are the physical, financial, information, and communications networks. Understanding the interdependencies and interrelationships of these networks is essential in planning for global distribution in support of operations. Assurance of the critical infrastructures that support each of the networks ensures continuity of global distribution.

(1) **Physical Network.** The physical network of the distribution system consists of the quantity, capacity, and capability of fixed structures and established facilities supporting distribution operations. It includes roads, railroads, structures (such as warehouses, depots, or storage facilities), ports, waterways, and pipelines. The physical network can be thought of as the skeletal and muscular structure of global distribution. General engineer capability allows global distribution to expand the capacity of the physical network (e.g., terminals, airfields, roads, waterways). Engineer reconnaissance provides information on the capacities of the physical system as well as identified potential barriers or bottlenecks.

See JP 3-35, Deployment and Redeployment Operations, *and JP 4-09,* Distribution Operations, *for more information.*

(2) **Transportation Infrastructure Assessment.** A transportation infrastructure assessment is key to understanding the capabilities and limitations of the urban operational area to support deployment operations. It serves as a basis to determine the forces, equipment, and materiel that must be deployed and facility upgrades required to enhance operations. A lesser developed, austere, or damaged infrastructure impedes deployment operations and may require an early deployment of support capabilities such as joint logistics over-the-shore, or engineer units. The combatant command engineer and staff prepare an engineer support plan (ESP) to ensure that essential engineering capabilities are identified and will be provided at the required locations and at the appropriate times to support the mobilization; deployment (movement and joint reception, staging, onward movement, and integration phases); employment; sustainment; and redeployment of the joint force in support of joint operations. The ESP establishes theater-level requirements for facilities, Class IV (construction materiel), and engineering capability in support of deployed US forces.

Additional information on ESP can be found in JP 3-34, Joint Engineer Operations, *and Appendix 6 to Annex D to Enclosure E of Chairman of the Joint Chiefs of Staff Manual (CJCSM) 3130.03,* Adaptive Planning and Execution (APEX) Planning Formats and Guidance.

3. Port Considerations

a. The planning and execution of port operations at the operational level requires a detailed analysis of a wide range of factors including:

(1) Overall concept of the operation.

(2) Logistic support requirements.

(3) Physical characteristics and layout of the port and/or beaches.

(4) Relative location of highway, rail, air, and inland waterway networks.

(5) Location of supported and supporting units.

(6) Required repair and rehabilitation of existing facilities.

(7) Requirement for new construction.

(8) Requirement for security, especially if HN support is not available.

(9) Required communications infrastructure, information systems to facilitate in-transit visibility, manifesting, and documentation requirements during vessel loading and discharge operations.

b. The probable location of port facilities within the urban area makes smooth operations problematic. The most significant factors influencing operations of the port are physical layout, the handling capabilities, the transportation infrastructure, and security.

c. Seaport adequacy is based on physical considerations that are often difficult to improve in the short term. Navigability, channel depths, numbers and sizes of ship berths, intermodal cargo handling equipment, and explosive handling limitations are significant factors that will affect materiel throughput. Another significant consideration is the impact of simultaneous commercial transportation, industrial operations, and other activities in the port area. Expansion of fixed port facilities by US forces requires a long lead time and significant resources.

4. Airfield Considerations

a. Air terminal operations involve numerous interdependent functions ranging from ensuring that sufficient airlift facilities are available to meeting any threat to operations.

b. Many large urban areas have relatively modern airports serving them, even if they are some distance from the central parts of the city. Other urban areas may be serviced by smaller, less modern facilities. Factors influencing airfield operations include the need to use the airfield for different types of flight operations (including civilian operations), the distance from joint force units and supply facilities, road capabilities, security, airfield capabilities, and adversary's capabilities to threaten airfield operations to include the use of CBRN weapons. Aircraft pose difficult decontamination challenges as compared to other transportation assets, and present more dire consequences than other transport modes if a large frame transport aircraft becomes contaminated. JFC plans must take into account these challenges in sustaining employment of aircraft into, within, and from contaminated areas.

For further information on logistic planning considerations in CBRN environments, see JP 3-11, Operations in Chemical, Biological, Radiological, and Nuclear Environments.

c. Factors such as runway length and weight bearing capability, taxiway systems, ramp space, materials handling equipment and personnel, maximum on the ground, aircraft servicing and maintenance, navigation aids, and communications systems affect maximum aircraft on the ground and throughput capacity of aerial ports. Again, a significant consideration in determining capabilities of an aerial port of debarkation (APOD) to support deployment and distribution operations is the effects of commercial transportation, industrial operations, and other activities in the port area. Construction or rehabilitation efforts can overcome some APOD shortcomings.

For additional information on planning development, refer to JP 5-0, Joint Operation Planning.

5. Security Considerations

a. Both port and airfield facilities will be susceptible to attack by conventional and unconventional means. As stationary targets, they are vulnerable to air, missile, and indirect fire attack, especially using CBRN munitions. Their size and probable locations, along with the presence of civilians, may encourage sabotage, terrorism, mining, and espionage.

b. The first step to providing security is threat assessment. Based on the assessed threat, the JFC can determine where to accept risks, where to focus protection efforts, and how much of the force should be devoted to protection of port and airfield facilities. Most terminals, ports, and airfields are physically laid out so that limited dispersion can be achieved within the boundaries of the port itself. In any case, dispersion does not permit maximum port use. The JFC increases his accepted risk to operations as he increases the use of established ports and airfields.

See JP 3-10, Joint Security Operations in Theater, *for more information.*

APPENDIX D
CONSIDERATIONS FOR AIRSPACE CONTROL IN AN URBAN ENVIRONMENT

1. General

a. Joint airspace control increases combat effectiveness by promoting the safe, efficient, and flexible use of airspace with minimum restraint upon airspace users, and includes coordinating, integrating, and regulating airspace to increase operational effectiveness. Effective airspace control reduces the risk of friendly fire, enhances air defense, and permits flexibility. Airspace control in an urban environment is conducted the same as in any other environment; however there are unique considerations.

b. The distinguishing features of urban airspace are compressed airspace and a unique three-dimensional ground environment. These factors increase planning and execution challenges, especially when in close proximity to friendly forces and civilians.

(1) Compressed airspace brings separate and diverse missions into close proximity. Fixed-wing, rotary-wing, UAS, ground fires, and ground scheme of maneuver must be integrated, deconflicted, and coordinated. Planning and execution becomes more difficult given the enemy's close proximity to friendly forces, protected sites, and civilians. For example, an aeromedical evacuation or an airdrop of supplies could be performed simultaneously with CAS missions protecting the unit being supported. Knowledge of other missions tasked for the same area is vital to avoid interference. Planning and deconfliction efforts must be undertaken to ensure all operations in the operational environment are coordinated and complement the overall objectives and commander's intent.

(2) The three-dimensional ground environment reaches into low-level airspace potentially used by fixed-wing and rotary-wing aircraft and UASs.

(3) The location of major airports in or near urban areas often puts the APOD inside the urban airspace.

(4) During operations in urban areas, a number of different types of aircraft may share the airspace—tactical aircraft, airlift assets, rotary-wing aircraft, UAS, and civilian aircraft.

2. Considerations

a. The JFC will normally designate a joint force air component commander (JFACC) to integrate the capabilities and C2 of joint air assets. The JFC also designates both the airspace control authority (ACA) and the area air defense commander (AADC).

For more information regarding the responsibilities and relationships of the JFACC, ACA, and AADC, see JP 3-30, Command and Control for Joint Air Operations; *JP 3-52,* Joint Airspace Control; *and JP 3-01,* Countering Air and Missile Threats.

b. The methods of airspace control may vary depending on the specific operation and the nature of the urban area. Methods range from full positive control to full procedural control of all air assets, or any effective combination of the two. Urban airspace control, in most instances, will require both positive and procedural control methods. Airspace coordinating measures must be developed to eliminate airspace conflicts. These measures must consider ongoing HN and foreign military airspace requirements, as well as UAS, SOF, other USG organizations, and IGO and NGO operations. The joint air tasking order (ATO)/airspace control order (ACO) aids deconfliction and synchronization of joint force aviation assets, which may include multinational air assets. The joint ATO/ACO must be made available for use by all participating forces to ensure greatest visibility on planned/ongoing airspace operations. Additionally, the use of a forward air controller (airborne) (FAC[A]) and/or tactical air coordinator (airborne) can assist in the management of urban airspace either in support of air control agencies or joint terminal attack controller (JTACs). Heightened awareness of other missions operating in and throughout the general area must be maintained.

c. The completed airspace control plan (ACP) will fully describe the airspace considerations, methods, and procedures that govern air and air defense operations in the urban area, including procedural airspace coordinating measures.

d. The control of urban airspace demands careful coordination to limit the potential conflict among aircraft needed for operations within that airspace. The ACA establishes airspace coordinating measures to facilitate this control.

3. Unmanned Aircraft Systems

Integration of UAS assets is important in effective urban operations. JFCs must deconflict UASs from other aviation assets, air-to-surface fires, and surface-to-surface fires during both intelligence collection and offensive missions. With the proliferation of tactical UASs, planners must pay close attention to integration and deconfliction within the objective area and ensure all units are informed of the plan. If present, the FAC(A) or JTAC must know the location and altitude of UASs within the objective area. Furthermore, when nontraditional strike platforms are re-tasked or transitioned from ISR to strike missions, a clear transfer of C2 must occur. Tactical air control parties (TACPs) are colocated with land maneuver forces. These teams have situational awareness of where UASs are employed. TACPs employ airspace coordination measures and deconflict aircraft flights with fire support plans and operations. Any conflicts with airspace for UAS and manned platforms will be resolved by airspace control procedures designated in the ACP.

For further details, refer to FM 3-06.1, Marine Corps Reference Publication (MCRP) 3-35.3A, NTTP 3-01.04, and Air Force Tactics, Techniques, and Procedures (Instruction) [AFTTP(I)] 3-2.29, Multi-Service Tactics, Techniques, and Procedures for Aviation Urban Operations.

APPENDIX E
MARITIME CONSIDERATIONS IN URBAN OPERATIONS

1. General

The significance of the littoral regions of the world cannot be overstated. Sixty percent of the politically significant urban areas around the world are located within 25 miles of a coastline while 75 percent are located within 150 miles of a coastline—80 percent of the world's population lives in close proximity to the sea. As urban areas continue to expand along the littorals and the corresponding potential for instability grows, the capabilities of maritime forces become ever more relevant. From deployment, through forcible entry and sustainment, to stability operations and redeployment, maritime forces play an important role in operations conducted in urban areas.

2. Port Security and Infrastructure Protection

a. In urban areas that also house key port facilities, security of the port, port-related infrastructure, and the riverine and seaward approaches to the port are important for numerous reasons. For example, sea ports facilitate the flow of follow-on forces and sustainment (e.g., reception, staging, onward movement, and integration, logistic distribution, evacuation, and maintenance). Additionally, ports support the flow of sustainment to the local population as well as the raw materials and finished products that support their economy, not to mention the large employment opportunities provided by the operating port and ancillary jobs base (e.g., warehousing, trucking). Both maritime expeditionary forces and United States Coast Guard (USCG) units can play a significant role in not only providing port and harbor security but in the development of HN capabilities. Specific details on capabilities and procedures can be found in respective Service publications.

b. United States Navy (USN) coastal riverine forces, comprised of maritime expeditionary security and riverine squadrons, support urban operations and augment port security and key infrastructure protection operations by denying an enemy or adversary the use of navigable waterways and rivers. The USN coastal riverine force combats sea-based terrorism and other illegal activities, such as transporting components of WMD, hijacking, piracy, and human trafficking. Coastal riverine units provide worldwide maritime and in-shore surveillance, security and force protection, ground defense, afloat defense, airfield/aircraft security, and a wide range of secondary tasks from detainee operations to law enforcement. USN coastal riverine forces operate in bays, rivers, harbors, and deltas in both littoral and inland regions. The introduction of USN coastal riverine forces requires an established forward operating base or a forward logistic site, which can be land- or sea-based. USCG forces may augment riverine forces with specialized units, such as port security units and maritime safety and security teams.

3. Seabasing in Support of Urban Operations

a. Maritime forces provide a distributed, persistent, sea-based presence without the increased destabilization that can be an unintended consequence of a heavy footprint ashore.

Seabasing sustainment, reserves, and administrative functions of the joint force may also enhance force protection.

b. As the "dominate phase" of urban operations transitions into the "stabilize" and "enable civil authority" phases, sea-based maritime forces continue to defend the seaward avenue of approach and can assist in training the local, indigenous security forces as well as the restoration of essential services (e.g., potable water, electricity, waste removal, basic medical care).

c. Discrete, tailored, less obtrusive support by sea-based forces minimizes potential resentment among the local populace, disparate HN and civil support organizations and reduces the risk of becoming a disruptive influence as the HN government reestablishes legitimacy in the eyes of the local population.

For more information, see Navy Warfare Publication (NWP) 3-62M/MCWP 3-31.7, Seabasing.

4. Coast Guard Support to Joint Urban Operations

a. The USCG is inherently flexible as both a military service and law enforcement agency within the Department of Homeland Security. The USCG supports DOD in its national defense role, across the forward regions, the global commons, the approaches, and within the US homeland. The USCG core competencies of waterways management, law enforcement, and littoral operations complement USN operations and enhance the capability of US forces to conduct unrestricted maritime operations worldwide.

b. The USCG brings unique skill sets and legal authorities which can facilitate support to JUOs. USCG units and boarding teams are highly trained in maritime law enforcement, maritime interception operations, as well as visit, board, search and seizure operations and tactics. USCG port security units, maritime safety and security teams, and law enforcement detachments are trained and authorized to make arrests at sea and can operate with the maritime expeditionary force. USCG units are also expert in broad scope defensive and offensive maritime operations ranging from protection of military and other high-value assets in ports, waterways and harbor approaches, to coastal sea control operations, to port operations, security, and defense which is conducted to ensure port and harbor areas are maintained free of hostile threats in seaports of embarkation and debarkation.

5. Other Support

a. In addition to the previous discussions, maritime forces can also be used to conduct or support intelligence activities, execute information-related capabilities, provide CAS and naval surface fire support and if required, a C2 platform in support of JUO.

b. With a large proportion of cities and urban areas located on or near the littorals, seabasing provides an additional capability to support JUOs. Seabasing is the deployment, assembly, command, projection, reconstitution, and re-employment of joint combat power from the sea without the reliance on land bases. It allows operational maneuver and assured access to the joint force, while significantly reducing the footprint ashore, thus avoiding the unwanted entanglements and vulnerabilities of a large force ashore in the HN territory. If the situation on the ground requires the JFC to minimize or optimize forces ashore in an urban area, the seabasing construct allows certain support functions to remain aboard ship. With a logistics tail safely in the sea base, the joint force is able to operate from international waters providing support to JUOs on land. Seabasing improves freedom of action, achieved through sea control, and increases the maneuver options for urban forces by reducing the need to protect elements such as C2 and logistic supplies. A sea base can be used to provide a floating forward operating base or a helicopter platform as was used in Haiti in 1994 and in the Persian Gulf in 1987-1988.

Intentionally Blank

APPENDIX F
REFERENCES

The development of JP 3-06 is based upon the following primary references:

1. **Department of Defense Publications**

   a. DOD Directive 3000.3, *Policy for Non-Lethal Weapons.*

   b. DOD Instruction 1322.27, *DOD Urban Training Facilities.*

   c. DOD Non-Lethal Weapons Program, *Non-Lethal Weapons (NLW) Reference Book.*

2. **Chairman of the Joint Chiefs of Staff Publications**

   a. CJCSI 3160.01, *No-Strike and The Collateral Damage Estimation Methodology.*

   b. CJCSM 3130.03, *Adaptive Planning and Execution (APEX) Planning Formats and Guidance.*

   c. JP 1, *Doctrine for the Armed Forces of the United States.*

   d. JP 1-0, *Joint Personnel Support.*

   e. JP 2-01.2 *Counterintelligence and Human Intelligence in Joint Operations (U).*

   f. JP 2-01.3, *Joint Intelligence Preparation of the Operational Environment.*

   g. JP 3-0, *Joint Operations.*

   h. JP 3-01, *Countering Air and Missile Threats.*

   i. JP 3-05, *Special Operations.*

   j. JP 3-07, *Stability Operations.*

   k. JP 3-07.3, *Peace Operations.*

   l. JP 3-08, *Interorganizational Coordination During Joint Operations.*

   m. JP 3-09, *Joint Fire Support.*

   n. JP 3-09.3, *Close Air Support.*

   o. JP 3-10, *Joint Security Operations in Theater.*

   p. JP 3-11, *Operations in Chemical, Biological, Radiological, and Nuclear Environments.*

q. JP 3-13, *Information Operations.*

r. JP 3-13.1, *Electronic Warfare.*

s. JP 3-13.2, *Military Information Support Operations.*

t. JP 3-13.4, *Military Deception.*

u. JP 3-14, *Space Operations.*

v. JP 3-15, *Barriers, Obstacles, and Mine Warfare for Joint Operations.*

w. JP 3-16, *Multinational Operations.*

x. JP 3-26, *Counterterrorism.*

y. JP 3-27, *Homeland Defense.*

z. JP 3-28, *Defense Support of Civil Authorities.*

aa. JP 3-29, *Foreign Humanitarian Assistance.*

bb. JP 3-30, *Command and Control for Joint Air Operations.*

cc. JP 3-31, *Command and Control for Joint Land Operations.*

dd. JP 3-33, *Joint Task Force Headquarters.*

ee. JP 3-34, *Joint Engineer Operations.*

ff. JP 3-35, *Deployment and Redeployment Operations.*

gg. JP 3-41, *Chemical, Biological, Radiological, and Nuclear Consequence Management.*

hh. JP 3-50, *Personnel Recovery.*

ii. JP 3-52, *Joint Airspace Control.*

jj. JP 3-57, *Civil-Military Operations.*

kk. JP 3-60, *Joint Targeting.*

ll. JP 3-61, *Public Affairs.*

mm. JP 3-63, *Detainee Operations.*

nn. JP 3-68, *Noncombatant Evacuation Operations.*

oo. JP 4-0, *Joint Logistics.*

pp. JP 4-01.2, *Sealift Support to Joint Operations.*

qq. JP 4-02, *Health Services.*

rr. JP 4-09, *Distribution Operations.*

ss. JP 5-0, *Joint Operation Planning.*

tt. JP 6-0, *Joint Communications System.*

3. Air Force Publication

Air Force Doctrine Document 3-24, *Irregular Warfare.*

4. Army Publications

a. Army Doctrine Reference Publication (ADRP) 3-05, *Special Operations.*

b. ADRP 3-07, *Stability.*

c. ATTP 3-06.11, *Combined Arms Operations in Urban Terrain.*

d. ATTP 3-34.80, *Geospatial Engineering.*

e. FM 2-01.3, *Intelligence Preparation of the Battlefield.*

f. FM 2-91.4, *Intelligence Support to Urban Operations.*

g. FM 3-05.30, *Psychological Operations.*

h. FM 3-06, *Urban Operations.*

i. FM 3-24, *Counterinsurgency.*

j. FM 3-57, *Civil Affairs Operations.*

k. FM 3-90.31, *Maneuver Enhancement Brigade Operations.*

l. FM 27-10, *The Law of Land Warfare.*

5. Marine Corps Publications

a. Marine Corps Doctrine Publication (MCDP) 1-0, *Marine Corps Operations.*

b. MCDP 3, *Expeditionary Operations.*

c. MCIA 2700-002-03, *Urban Generic Information Requirements Handbook (UGIRH).*

d. MCIA, *Urban Warfare Study: City Case Studies Compilation,* February 1999.

e. MCWP 3-35.3, *Military Operations on Urbanized Terrain.*

6. Navy Publications

a. Naval Doctrinal Publication 1, *Naval Warfare.*

b. NWP 3-10, *Maritime Expeditionary Security Operations.*

c. NTTP 3-06.1, *Riverine Operations.*

d. NTTP 3-10.1, *Naval Coastal Warfare Operations.*

7. Miscellaneous Publications

a. 10th Mountain Division (LI), Somalia. *US Army Forces: After Action Report: Summary.* Fort Drum: 10th Mountain Division, Headquarters. June 1993.

b. Adams, Thomas. "Intervention in Haiti: Lessons Relearned." *Military Review.* September/October 1996: pp. 45–56.

c. Air Land Sea Bulletin 2008-1, January 2008 *MOUT Military Operations in Urban Terrain.*

d. Air Land Sea Bulletin 2011-2, May 2011, *Aviation in Urban Operations.*

e. Allard, Kenneth. *Somalia Operations: Lessons Learned.* Ft. McNair: National Defense University Press. 1995.

f. "The Balkan Air Campaign Study: Part II." *Air Power Journal.* Vol. XI, No. 3, Fall 1997: pp. 4-24.

g. Celestan, MAJ Gregory J., USA. *Wounded Bear: The Ongoing Russian Military Operation in Chechnya.* Center for Army Lessons Learned, August 1996.

h. Collins, John M. *Military Geography.* National Defense University Press: Washington, DC, 1998.

i. Cooling, Norman L. *Shaping the Battlespace to Win the Street Fight.* United States Marine Corps Command and Staff College, 1999. (unpublished thesis)

j. DOD, *Joint Urban Operations Joint Integrating Concept*, 23 July 2007.

k. Doerrer, Eric A. "Civil Affairs in Haiti." *Military Review.* March/April 1996: pp. 73–79.

l. Finch, MAJ Raymond C., III, USA. *Why the Russian Military Failed in Chechnya.* Center For Army Lessons Learned.

m. Gerwehr, Scott, and Russell W. Glenn, *Unweaving the Web: Deception and Adaptation in Future Urban Operations*, RAND, 2003.

n. Glenn, Russell W. *An Attack on Duffer's Downtown.* RAND, 2001.

o. Glenn, Russell W. *The Art of Darkness: Deception and Urban Operations.* 2000.

p. Glenn, Russell W. *Combat in Hell: A Consideration of Constrained Urban Warfare.* RAND, 1996.

q. Glenn, Russell W., and Gina Kingston, *Urban Battle: Command in the Twenty-First Century*, RAND, 2005.

r. Glenn, Russell W. *Urban Combat is Complex*, RAND, 2002.

s. Glenn, Russell W. *Marching Under Darkening Skies: The American Military and the Impending Urban Operations Threat*, RAND, 1998.

t. Glenn, Russell W. *Managing Complexity During Military Urban Operations: Visualizing the Elephant*, RAND, 2004.

u. Glenn, Russell W., Jamison Jo Medby, Scott Gerwehr, Frederick J. Gellert, and Andrew O'Donnell. *Honing the Keys to the City: Refining the United States Marine Corps Reconnaissance Force for Urban Ground Combat Operations*, RAND, 2003.

v. Glenn, Russell W., Randall Steeb, and John Matsumura. *Corralling the Trojan Horse: A Proposal for Improving US Urban Operations Preparedness in the Period 2000-2025*, RAND, 2001.

w. Glenn, Russell W., Christopher Paul, Todd C. Helmus, and Paul Steinberg. *"People Make the City," Executive Summary: Joint Urban Operations Observations and Insights from Afghanistan and Iraq,* RAND, 2007.

x. Glenn, Russell W., Steven Hartman, and Scott Gerwehr. *Urban Combat Service Support Operations: The Shoulders of Atlas*, RAND, 2004.

y. Glenn, Russell W., Jody Jacobs, Brian Nichiporuk, Christopher Paul, Barbara Raymond, Randall Steeb, and Harry J. Thie. *Preparing for the Proven Inevitable: An Urban Operations Training Strategy for America's Joint Force*, RAND, 2006.

z. Glenn, Russell W. *Heavy Matter: Urban Operations' Density of Challenges.* RAND, 2000.

aa. Grau, Lester W. "Changing Russian Urban Tactics: The Aftermath of the Battle for Grozny." *INSS Strategic Forum,* No. 38, July 1995.

bb. Grau, Lester W., ed. *The Bear Went Over the Mountain.* Washington, DC: National Defense University Press, 1996.

cc. Grau, Lester W., and Dr. William A. Jorgensen. "Handling the Wounded in a Counter-Guerrilla War: the Soviet/Russian Experience in Afghanistan and Chechnya." *US Army Medical Department Journal,* January/February 1998.

dd. Grau, Lester W. "Russian Urban Tactics: Lessons from the Battle for Grozny." *National Defense University's Strategic Forum.* Institute for National Strategic Studies.

ee. Grau, LTC Lester W., USA (Ret.), and LTC Timothy L. Thomas USA (Ret.). "Soft Log and Concrete Canyons: Russian Urban Logistics in Grozny." *Marine Corps Gazette,* Vol. 83, Issue 10 (October 1999): pp. 67-75.

ff. Helmus, Todd C., and Russell W. Glenn. *Steeling the Mind: Combat Stress Reactions and Their Implications for Urban Warfare*, RAND, 2005.

gg. Helmus, Todd C., Christopher Paul, and Russell W. Glenn. *Enlisting Madison Avenue: The Marketing Approach to Earning Popular Support in Theaters of Operation*, RAND, 2007.

hh. *Handbook for Joint Urban Operations.*

ii. *Joint Military Operations Historical Collection.*

jj. Joint Special Operations University Report 09-8, September 2009, *Irregular Warfare: Brazil's Fight Against Criminal Urban Guerrilla.*

kk. Manwaring, Max G. *Street Gangs: The New Urban Insurgency*, Strategic Studies Institute, US Army War College, March 2005.

ll. Matthews, M. *Operation AL FAJR: A Study in Army and Marine Corps Joint Operations*, Combat Studies Institute, 2006.

mm. McLaurin, R. D., and R. Miller. *Urban Counterinsurgency: Case Studies and Implications for US Military Forces*, Abbott Associates, Inc., October 1989.

nn. Medby, Jamison Jo, and Russell W. Glenn. *Street Smart Intelligence: Preparation of the Battlefield for Urban Operations*, RAND, 2002.

oo. Mordica, George J., II. *It's a Dirty Business, But Somebody Has to Do It (Urban Combat).* Center for Army Lessons Learned.

pp. Owen, Robert C., Lieutenant Colonel, USAF. "The Balkan Air Campaign Study: Part I." *Air Power Journal,* Vol. XI, No. 2, Summer 1997: pp. 4–24.

qq. Robertson, William G. (General Editor). *Block by Block: The Challenges of Urban Operations*, Combat Studies Institute, 2003.

rr. Scales, MG Robert H., Jr., USA. *Future Warfare.* US Army War College, 1999.

ss. Schnaubelt, Christopher M. "The 1992 Los Angeles Riots, Lessons in Command and Control from the Los Angeles Riots." *Parameters*, Summer 1997: pp. 88-109.

tt. Shelton, Lieutenant General H. Hugh, and Lieutenant Colonel Timothy D. Vane. "Winning the Information War in Haiti." *Military Review*, November/December 1995: pp. 3-9.

uu. Simmons, Dean, Phillip Gould, Verena Vomastic, and Phillip Walsh. "Air Operations over Bosnia." *United States Naval Institute Proceedings,* May 1997.

vv. Spiller, Rojer J. *Sharp Corners: Urban Operations at Century's End,* US Army Command and General Staff College Press, 2001.

ww. Thomas, Timothy L. "The Battle of Grozny: Deadly Classroom for Urban Combat." *Parameters* (Summer 1999): pp. 87-102.

xx. Thomas, Timothy L. "The Caucasus Conflict and Russian Security: The Russian Armed Forces Confront Chechnya." *Journal of Slavic Military Studies,* Vol. 8, No. 2 (June 1995): pp. 233-290.

yy. Thomas, Timothy L. "The Caucasus Conflict and Russian Security: The Russian Armed Forces Confront Chechnya III. The Battle for Grozny, 1–16 January 1995." *Journal of Slavic Military Studies,* Vol. 10 (March 1997), pp. 50–108.

zz. US Special Operations Command Pub 3-33, *Conventional Forces and Special Operations Forces Integration and Interoperability Handbook and Checklist.*

aaa. Vick, Allen, et. al., *Aerospace Operations in Urban Environments: Exploring New Concepts,* RAND, 2000.

8. Multi-Service Publications

a. ATTP 3-04.15 (FM 3-04.15)/MCRP 3-42.1A/NTTP 3-55.14/Air Force Tactics, Techniques, and Procedures (AFTTP) 3-2.64, *Multi-Service Tactics, Techniques, and Procedures for Unmanned Aircraft Systems.*

b. FM 3-06.1/MCRP 3-35.3A/NTTP 3-01.04/AFTTP 3-2.29, *Multi-Service Tactics, Techniques, and Procedures for Aviation Urban Operations.*

c. FM 3-22.40/MCWP 3-15.8/NTTP 3-07.3.2/AFTTP(I) 3-2.45, *Multi-Service Tactics, Techniques, and Procedures for the Tactical Employment of Nonlethal Weapons.*

9. Joint Courseware

a. Introduction to Joint Urban Operations Course, J3OP-US017, http://jko.jten.mil/.

b. Joint Urban Operations for Joint Force Commander and Staff, J3OP-US120, http://jko.jten.mil/.

10. Internet Resources

a. Ambush in Mogadishu: http://www.pbs.org/wgbh/pages/frontline/shows/ambush.

b. City Population: http://www.citypopulation.de/cities.html.

c. Joint Urban Operations Education Program Community of Interest, https://www.us.army.mil/suite/page/426393.

d. Universal Joint Task OP 1.2.8 – Conduct Joint Urban Operations (JUO) https://jdeis.js.mil/jdeis/index.jsp?pindex=81&id=3284.

e. Unrestricted Warfare Analysis Center, https://www.intelink.gov/sites/uwac/default.aspx.

APPENDIX G
ADMINISTRATIVE INSTRUCTIONS

1. User Comments

Users in the field are highly encouraged to submit comments on this publication to: Joint Staff J-7, Deputy Director, Joint Education and Doctrine, ATTN: Joint Doctrine Analysis Division, 116 Lake View Parkway, Suffolk, VA 23435-2697. These comments should address content (accuracy, usefulness, consistency, and organization), writing, and appearance.

2. Authorship

The lead agent for this publication is the US Army. The Joint Staff doctrine sponsor for this publication is the Director for Force Structure, Resources, and Assessment (J-8).

3. Supersession

This publication supersedes JP 3-06, 08 November 2009, *Joint Urban Operations.*

4. Change Recommendations

a. Recommendations for urgent changes to this publication should be submitted:

TO: JOINT STAFF WASHINGTON DC//J7-JE&D//

b. Routine changes should be submitted electronically to the Deputy Director, Joint Education and Doctrine, ATTN: Joint Doctrine Analysis Division, 116 Lake View Parkway, Suffolk, VA 23435-2697, and info the lead agent and the Director for Joint Force Development, J-7/JE&D.

c. When a Joint Staff directorate submits a proposal to the CJCS that would change source document information reflected in this publication, that directorate will include a proposed change to this publication as an enclosure to its proposal. The Services and other organizations are requested to notify the Joint Staff J-7 when changes to source documents reflected in this publication are initiated.

5. Distribution of Publications

Local reproduction is authorized, and access to unclassified publications is unrestricted. However, access to and reproduction authorization for classified JPs must be IAW DOD Manual 5200.01, Volume 1, *DOD Information Security Program: Overview, Classification, and Declassification,* and DOD Manual 5200.01, Volume 3, *DOD Information Security Program: Protection of Classified Information.*

6. Distribution of Electronic Publications

a. Joint Staff J-7 will not print copies of JPs for distribution. Electronic versions are available on JDEIS at https://jdeis.js.mil (NIPRNET) and http://jdeis.js.smil.mil (SIPRNET), and on the JEL at http://www.dtic.mil/doctrine (NIPRNET).

b. Only approved JPs are releasable outside the combatant commands, Services, and Joint Staff. Release of any classified JP to foreign governments or foreign nationals must be requested through the local embassy (Defense Attaché Office) to DIA, Defense Foreign Liaison/IE-3, 200 MacDill Blvd., Joint Base Anacostia-Bolling, Washington, DC 20340-5100.

c. JEL CD-ROM. Upon request of a joint doctrine development community member, the Joint Staff J-7 will produce and deliver one CD-ROM with current JPs. This JEL CD-ROM will be updated not less than semi-annually and when received can be locally reproduced for use within the combatant commands, Services, and combat support agencies.

GLOSSARY
PART I—ACRONYMS AND ABBREVIATIONS

AAA	antiaircraft artillery
AADC	area air defense commander
ACA	airspace control authority
ACO	airspace control order
ACP	airspace control plan
ADRP	Army doctrine reference publication
AFTTP	Air Force tactics, techniques, and procedures
AFTTP(I)	Air Force tactics, techniques, and procedures (instruction)
AO	area of operations
AOI	area of interest
APOD	aerial port of debarkation
ATO	air tasking order
ATTP	Army tactics, techniques, and procedures
BDA	battle damage assessment
C2	command and control
CA	civil affairs
CAO	civil affairs operations
CAS	close air support
CBRN	chemical, biological, radiological, and nuclear
CCDR	combatant commander
CI	counterintelligence
CID	combat identification
CJCSI	Chairman of the Joint Chiefs of Staff instruction
CJCSM	Chairman of the Joint Chiefs of Staff manual
CMO	civil-military operations
CMOC	civil-military operations center
COA	course of action
COG	center of gravity
CONOPS	concept of operations
DA	direct action
DOD	Department of Defense
DOS	Department of State
DP	decisive point
ESP	engineer support plan
FAC(A)	forward air controller (airborne)
FCM	foreign consequence management
FHA	foreign humanitarian assistance
FHP	force health protection

FID	foreign internal defense
FM	field manual (Army)
GEOINT	geospatial intelligence
GIBCO	geospatial intelligence base for contingency operations
GPS	Global Positioning System
HN	host nation
HUMINT	human intelligence
IED	improvised explosive device
IGO	intergovernmental organization
IO	information operations
IPI	indigenous populations and institutions
ISR	intelligence, surveillance, and reconnaissance
JFACC	joint force air component commander
JFC	joint force commander
JFLCC	joint force land component commander
JIPOE	joint intelligence preparation of the operational environment
JNCC	joint network operations control center
JOA	joint operations area
JP	joint publication
JTAC	joint terminal attack controller
JTF	joint task force
JUO	joint urban operation
LOC	line of communications
LOE	line of effort
LOO	line of operation
LOS	line of sight
MCDP	Marine Corps doctrine publication
MCIA	Marine Corps Intelligence Activity
MCRP	Marine Corps reference publication
MCWP	Marine Corps warfighting publication
MEA	munitions effectiveness assessment
MIS	military information support
MISO	military information support operations
MOE	measure of effectiveness
MOP	measure of performance
NEO	noncombatant evacuation operation
NGA	National Geospatial-Intelligence Agency
NGO	nongovernmental organization

NTTP	Navy tactics, techniques, and procedures
NWP	Navy warfare publication
OSINT	open-source intelligence
PA	public affairs
PMESII	political, military, economic, social, information, and infrastructure
PR	personnel recovery
PRC	populace and resources control
ROE	rules of engagement
RUF	rules for the use of force
SAR	search and rescue
SecDef	Secretary of Defense
SIGINT	signals intelligence
SJA	staff judge advocate
SOF	special operations forces
SR	special reconnaissance
TACP	tactical air control party
TIM	toxic industrial material
TST	time-sensitive target
TTP	tactics, techniques, and procedures
UAS	unmanned aircraft system
UGIRH	*Urban Generic Information Requirements Handbook*
USAID	United States Agency for International Development
USCG	United States Coast Guard
USG	United States Government
USN	United States Navy
WMD	weapons of mass destruction

PART II—TERMS AND DEFINITIONS

joint urban operations. Joint operations planned and conducted on, or against objectives within a topographical complex and its adjacent natural terrain, where man-made construction or the density of population are the dominant features. Also called **JUOs.** (Approved for incorporation into JP 1-02.)

key facilities list. None. (Approved for removal from JP 1-02.)

objective area. A geographical area, defined by competent authority, within which is located an objective to be captured or reached by the military forces. Also called **OA.** (Approved for incorporation into JP 1-02.)

turning movement. A variation of the envelopment in which the attacking force passes around or over the enemy's principal defensive positions to secure objectives deep in the enemy's rear to force the enemy to abandon his position or divert major forces to meet the threat. (JP 1-02. SOURCE: JP 3-06)

urban triad. None. (Approved for removal from JP 1-02.)

JOINT DOCTRINE PUBLICATIONS HIERARCHY

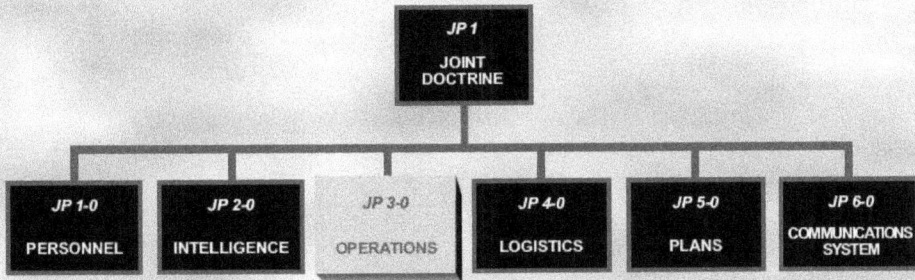

```
                              ┌─────────────┐
                              │    JP 1     │
                              │    JOINT    │
                              │  DOCTRINE   │
                              └─────────────┘
```

JP 1-0	JP 2-0	JP 3-0	JP 4-0	JP 5-0	JP 6-0
PERSONNEL	INTELLIGENCE	OPERATIONS	LOGISTICS	PLANS	COMMUNICATIONS SYSTEM

All joint publications are organized into a comprehensive hierarchy as shown in the chart above. **Joint Publication (JP) 3-06** is in the **Operations** series of joint doctrine publications. The diagram below illustrates an overview of the development process:

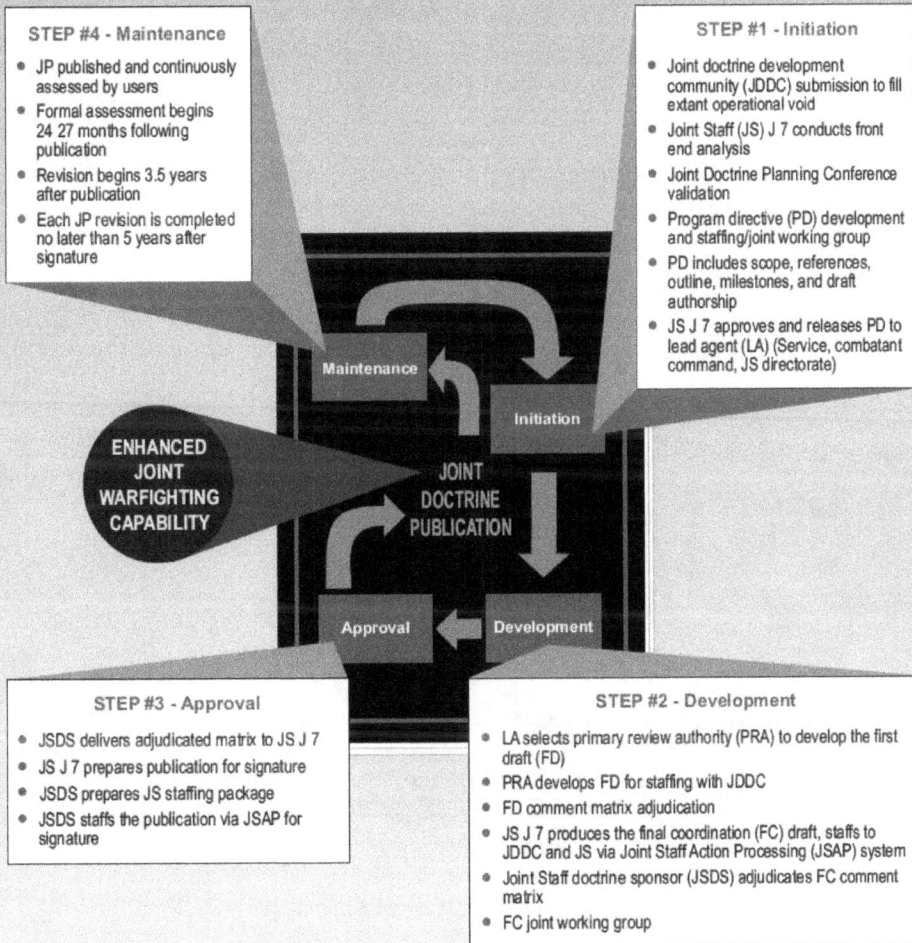

STEP #4 - Maintenance

- JP published and continuously assessed by users
- Formal assessment begins 24 27 months following publication
- Revision begins 3.5 years after publication
- Each JP revision is completed no later than 5 years after signature

STEP #1 - Initiation

- Joint doctrine development community (JDDC) submission to fill extant operational void
- Joint Staff (JS) J 7 conducts front end analysis
- Joint Doctrine Planning Conference validation
- Program directive (PD) development and staffing/joint working group
- PD includes scope, references, outline, milestones, and draft authorship
- JS J 7 approves and releases PD to lead agent (LA) (Service, combatant command, JS directorate)

Maintenance

Initiation

ENHANCED JOINT WARFIGHTING CAPABILITY

JOINT DOCTRINE PUBLICATION

Approval

Development

STEP #3 - Approval

- JSDS delivers adjudicated matrix to JS J 7
- JS J 7 prepares publication for signature
- JSDS prepares JS staffing package
- JSDS staffs the publication via JSAP for signature

STEP #2 - Development

- LA selects primary review authority (PRA) to develop the first draft (FD)
- PRA develops FD for staffing with JDDC
- FD comment matrix adjudication
- JS J 7 produces the final coordination (FC) draft, staffs to JDDC and JS via Joint Staff Action Processing (JSAP) system
- Joint Staff doctrine sponsor (JSDS) adjudicates FC comment matrix
- FC joint working group

www.ingramcontent.com/pod-product-compliance
Lightning Source LLC
Chambersburg PA
CBHW080510110426
42742CB00017B/3063